THE GREAT UNIVERSE OF KOTA

THE
GREAT UNIVERSE
OF KOTA

*Stress, Change and Mental Disorder
in an Indian Village*

★

G. M. CARSTAIRS

and

R. L. KAPUR

UNIVERSITY OF CALIFORNIA PRESS

Berkeley and Los Angeles

University of California Press
Berkeley and Los Angeles, California

ISBN 0-520-03024-9
LC 75-13151

Printed in Great Britain

CONTENTS

FOREWORD

This essay into the field of Culture and Mental Health differs from most of its predecessors (with one notable exception) in that it is not the work of a Western-trained psychiatrist, observing and interpreting the behaviour of an alien people. The exception is, of course, the study *Psychiatric Disorder among the Yoruba*, a joint undertaking by the American, Alexander H. Leighton, and the Nigerian, Thomas A. Lambo, each assisted by teams of co-workers from their respective cultures.

In the present study, there has also been a collaboration between scientists and field workers drawn from two cultures: we, the authors, have ourselves encountered not so much the clash between two cultures as a commingling of their respective influences in our own experience. Both of us were born and spent our formative years in India. Thereafter, Morris Carstairs travelled to Scotland, the land of his forefathers, in order to complete his schooling and his training in medicine, psychiatry and anthropology, returning to India only after many years in order to carry out anthropological field work in Rajasthan. During the past twenty years he has paid numerous visits to the land of his birth in his capacity as a teacher and researcher in social psychiatry. Ravi Kapur, on the other hand, completed his medical studies and his psychiatric training in India, and then spent more than five years in Edinburgh, rapidly assimilating the mores of British academic life, into which he entered fully. He learned the techniques of epidemiological research and practised them in a PhD study of factors related to student failures at Edinburgh University before returning to India to deploy the same skills in his capacity as Field Director of the present project.

This study differs in one important respect from that of Leighton and Lambo, which demonstrated the replication, in a different language and culture, of a study whose techniques and instruments of inquiry had been painstakingly developed in North America. The present study was planned, in its broad outlines, by both authors working together in Edinburgh; but its instruments were developed in South India, in the language of the people to be studied, and its methods of inquiry were tested in pilot studies in the same linguistic area. The major role in all this field work, and in the statistical analysis of the results of the final survey, was performed by Ravi Kapur.

Both authors would like to acknowledge their debt to a number of colleagues who contributed to the study, in particular to Malavika Kapur who gave substantial help in the development of the Indian Psychiatric Schedule, and to the research assistants who took part in the field survey: Dr Sayeed Ahmed, Mr K. N. K. Eshwar, Miss V. Lalitha and Miss R. Kshama, and the invaluable village guide, Guruva Marakala. Special thanks are due to Dr Norman Kreitman, Director of the M.R.C. Unit for Research on Epidemiological Aspects of Psychiatry, in the Edinburgh University Department of Psychiatry, which was the organisational base of the study throughout its course. Thanks are also due to the All India Institute of Mental Health, Bangalore, and to Kasturba Medical College, Manipal, both of which provided generous help with accommodation and other facilities.

The authors benefited from many suggestions and constructive criticisms contributed by Norman Kreitman, and other members of his Research Unit, notably Dorothy Buglass, Pat Dugard and John Clarke. Our Indian colleagues, Drs R. M. Varma, N. N. Wig and J. S. Neki, have also been generous with their help and advice; but we owe an especial debt to yet another distinguished Indian psychiatrist, Dr N. C. Surya, formerly Director of the All India Institute of Mental Health, Bangalore, and now a member of Sri Aurobindo Ashram, Pondicherry. As teacher, colleague and friend, Dr Surya has been, and still remains, a constant source of inspiration, encouragement and—let us admit it—sometimes of irritation; but only of the kind which spurs one to renewed, and more productive, exertions.

As in all studies of this kind, a special debt of gratitude is due to the members of the community which we studied. No pseudonyms have been used to disguise the location of the study, or the communities involved; but we have refrained from identifying any of our hundreds of individual informants, in order to respect the confidentiality of their communications with us. For more than two years they showed great patience with our inquiries, and unfailing co-operation whenever this was needed. Not least of their contributions was to provide us with the title of this book. In village gossip we frequently heard reference to 'Kota Mahajagat'; in thus describing their extended village as a 'Great Universe' they were partly engaging in self-mockery but partly expressing their pride in belonging to a complex social network which represents in microcosm the vast variegated society of rural India as a whole.

It should perhaps be pointed out that the village of Kota bears no relation to the small tribal community of the same name which has been studied by the anthropologist David Mandlebaum (1938, 1955, 1956; 1970). The latter is one of four tribal groups—the others being the pastoral Todas, the Korumba sorcerers and the Badaga cultivators—who inhabit the Nilgiri plateau in the state of Tamil Nadu. In contrast, with those peoples, who have emerged only during the last two generations from centuries of relative isolation, the populous coastal village with which we are concerned has a long history of involvement with the wider Hindu society of South India.

This study was made possible through a generous grant from the Foundations Fund for Research in Psychiatry, to whom we are glad to acknowledge our debt of gratitude.

G. M. CARSTAIRS
University of York
England

R. L. KAPUR
National Institute for
Mental Health and
Neurosciences
Bangalore
India

CULTURE AND MENTAL DISORDER

In the early years of this century three different views were emerging among Western students of normal and abnormal psychology with regard to the nature and distribution of mental disorder in so-called 'primitive' societies. Influenced by Rousseau's concept of the Noble Savage, some believed that mental disorder was the result of the restrictions and stresses imposed by modern civilisation and thus would be rare in peoples not yet affected by industrialisation. Eminent pioneers including Freud and Maudsley shared this view. Subsequent anthropological research has, however, shown that mental disturbance occurs in every society, without exception, but varies in its frequency of occurrence in different societies: hence, attention has turned towards a study of cultural factors which are associated with higher or lower prevalence rates for mental disorder.

There were others, like Kraepelin, who believed that mental illness was primarily due to biological factors which cut across cultural boundaries and hence would be encountered in all societies. His immediate successors in German psychiatry were especially interested in trying to demonstrate the importance of heredity in these disorders. A third group took the strange step of judging alien cultures in terms of beliefs and values current in the West and then describing their findings in psychiatric terminology. For example, Kroeber, an eminent social anthropologist, categorised all societies in which belief in the supernatural was prevalent as 'paranoid cultures'.

While hardly anyone would subscribe to the last view nowadays, a considerable rapprochement has occurred between the respective protagonists of the first two. This coming together has followed the greater understanding we now have both of the phenomenon of mental disorder and of the nature of primitive societies.

Most psychiatrists would agree that 'mental disorder' is a collective term for many different conditions, each differing in their causation and each presenting a characteristic symptomatology. In some conditions a disease process of the brain can be clearly demonstrated. There are others where a biochemical disturbance of genetic origin has been identified, and yet others in which similar processes are strongly suspected. There are still others which are believed to be ascribable to the breakdown of a vulnerable personality in the face of stress or conflict. This vulnerability of the personality is itself thought to be the result of an interaction between one's genetic heritage and the stresses one is exposed to, during crucial periods of personality development. Even for those conditions where the cause is mainly biological, environmental factors can alter the presentation and the course of the disorder. There is thus a constant interplay between biological and environmental factors, the former playing a more dominant role in some and the latter in other psychiatric conditions. From this position it can be argued that those mental disorders which are largely determined by biological factors to which all mankind is susceptible will be found to occur at a roughly similar rate in widely different cultural settings, while those in which experiential factors are more important, will be encountered in greater numbers in those cultures which impose relatively greater amounts of emotional stress on their members.

While psychiatrists were engaged in developing an eclectic view of the nature of mental disorder, anthropologists were discovering that earlier assumptions about primitive societies being stress-free were rather naive and that in fact the experience of frustration and conflict is an inescapable element in the human condition everywhere. Different societies impose different kinds of restrictions on their members, and it is not always easy to say which restrictions are the more stressful. Further, though some societies are more restrictive than others, there is as much variation in this respect among the so-called primitive cultures as one finds between them as a group and the Western cultures.

Another issue relevant to the discussion is that of cultural change. There is evidence that the processes of technological advance and industrialisation which are going on all over the world are accompanied by rapid alterations in the traditional ways of life which, according to some, must be stressful. Whether rapid cultural change inevitably produces stress and if so, whether this stress affects everyone in the group or only those with vulnerable personalities has, however, yet to be proved. It is also arguable that rapid technological and social change is now a world-wide phenomenon, affecting already advanced societies almost as strongly as it does the developing countries.

The original question, whether mental disorder is equally distributed all over the world or is peculiar to Western civilisation, can now be rephrased in the following set of questions: Do cultures differ in the distribution of mental disorders? Which disorders are, and which are not, particularly affected by cultural variations? What kinds of stresses do particular cultures impose on their members? Are particular kinds of stresses conducive to specific mental disorders? Is rapid cultural change conducive to mental disorder? What types of cultural change are more 'toxic' to mental health than others?

These are important questions because answers to them would clarify the relative significance of environmental factors in the causation of mental disorder. Such knowledge, besides being of interest in its own right, would be an extremely valuable guide for future therapeutic and preventive programmes. As we shall see, however, cross-cultural research in psychiatry presents some formidable difficulties.

One might assume that such questions could be answered by studying the relative frequency of mental disorder in two cultures which are known to differ in the nature and degree of stress they impose on their members. Such research has, in fact, been going on for a good many years but the various studies have provided very little firm evidence one way or the other.

Scientifically rigorous cross-cultural comparisons of psychiatric disorders are bedevilled by one major, indeed almost insuperable methodological difficulty, and by a host of only slightly less formidable obstacles.

Before proceeding, in subsequent chapters, to describe how these problems were tackled in the study which we carried out in three contrasting communities in South India, and to discuss our findings, it will be necessary to indicate the nature of these methodological difficulties in some detail.

The key problem of cross-cultural comparisons of mental disorders

It stands to reason that if the frequency of occurrence of an entity in two different situations is to be compared the entity should be similarly defined in the two situations. This is very difficult to accomplish in the case of mental disorder since the very concept of what is psychologically normal or abnormal is dependent on the beliefs, values and codes of human interaction which characterise a given cultural group, and therefore varies from one group to another. Each culture has its own criteria of reality, and a symptom regarded as indicative of mental abnormality in one may not be so regarded in the other. A psychiatric symptom may be simply defined as a mental state which is perceived as odd, distressful or harmful by the person suffering from it, or by those around him, or both. However, what is odd, distressful and harmful to members of one cultural group may not be so regarded by members of another one. Certainly there are people who would be considered mad in any cultural setting; but there are others who show patterns of thinking, mood, speech, attitude, perception and behaviour perfectly acceptable in one but not so in another culture. A belief in spirits, considered perfectly normal in one group, becomes a delusion when expressed by a person belonging to another more 'rational' culture. A degree of rebelliousness which is acceptable as normal in a Western adolescent can be seen as very distressful and odd when displayed by his counterpart in an orthodox Hindu family.

The further apart cultures are in their beliefs and values, the greater will be the difference in their concepts of mental abnormality. Researchers have tried to overcome this difficulty by taking standard operational definitions for the various psychiatric symptoms, building objective questionnaires based on these definitions, laboriously translating and retranslating the questions from one language to another, and finally training investigators in different settings to use the questionnaires similarly. Such an artificial ritual to attain uniformity can hardly mask the fundamental question—from whose point of view is this questionnaire 'objective', that of culture A or culture B? Again, in an area where culturally determined beliefs and value orientations enter into the very definition of what is normal and abnormal, how scientific is it to be 'objective' in this fashion?

Even if one could develop a comparable method for estimating mental disorder and one group was found to have a higher case rate than the other, the next problem would be to interpret the significance of such a finding in terms of the cultural differences. Unfortunately, though one can intuitively feel these differences, the techniques of socio-anthropological observation and analysis are not sufficiently developed to measure those subtle parameters which are crucial, whereas those which *can* be measured are generally of little relevance to the study of mental disorder.

It is for these reasons that Kessel (1965) doubted the validity of international comparisons in psychiatric epidemiology. He recommended that any such comparisons should be limited to cultures which have similar concepts of mental disorder, which share a common language, and which are generally similar except on some striking and measurable parameters, the effect of which is under investigation. Such cultures are not easy to come by!

Problems of case detection

One problem which is not limited to cross-cultural comparisons but which plagues psychiatric epidemiology in general, is that of determining the case rate in the general population. Hospital admission statistics are obviously of limited use because they are affected by a number of factors which have nothing to do with the 'real' case rate—such as the facilities available and the willingness of the people to make use of these facilities. In many parts of the world there are no psychiatric hospitals at all. In other places, even when psychiatric facilities have been made available, people, conditioned by their beliefs about the causation of mental abnormality, would rather consult astrologers, mediums or priests than go to a doctor. Finally, even where the facilities are available and an admission to a hospital is considered necessary, some patients might be deterred from going to them because of the distance or the expense involved in travelling and paying for the services.

In order to obtain a true measure of the prevalence of mental disorders, one must carry out a population survey, but such attempts meet with another set of difficulties. There are no absolute, standard criteria for defining a psychiatric case in the general population. There is no germ which can be indisputably demonstrated under a microscope, and there are no precise laboratory investigations which would distinguish a person suffering from mental disorder from one who is not. In psychiatry, the diagnosis of a disorder is arrived at through clinical assessment, and so crude is this method that different experts often disagree about their decisions. Disagreements are less marked at the level of observation of symptoms, but become greater at the next stages, of interpretation or allocation to a particular diagnostic category.

Inter-observer variations can arise because a person who is being interviewed may respond differently to different interviewers; or two observers may differ in their ability to establish the necessary rapport with their informant. The observers might also be influenced in their perception by their own mental state at the time of inquiry —for example by their own emotional need to see or not to see a disturbing feature.

Once having observed a particular phenomenon, different investigators may differ in their relative tendency to consider it abnormal, and hence to assign the person who exhibits it to a particular diagnostic category. Variability at this last step is further compounded by the unsatisfactory manner in which mental disorders are classified at the present state of our knowledge.

According to one study a pair of psychiatrists reached agreement on the diagnostic category in only 65 per cent of cases (Kreitman *et al.*, 1961). According to another study, when 538 female patients were admitted to three different wards at random, the diagnosis of schizophrenia was given to 68, 29 and 22 per cent (Pasamanick *et al.*, 1959) of the patients in the three wards respectively. In such a random allocation there was no reason why one ward should get more schizophrenics than the others. Obviously, the doctors in charge differed in their readiness to diagnose schizophrenia. In another recent well-designed comparative study it was found that the same group of patients were diagnosed as schizophrenic much more often by a group of American psychiatrists than by a corresponding group of British psychiatrists (Cooper *et al.*, 1972).

It is because of the unreliability of the diagnostic procedure that psychiatric surveys based on clinical assessment, however comprehensive they may be, must be considered unsatisfactory. The unsatisfactory nature of this approach is demonstrated by the fact that different studies carried out in very similar populations have produced case rates of mental disorder varying from 16·7 to as much as 333 per thousand!

Disappointed with the clinical approach, some workers have employed objective questionnaires and have trained the investigators taking part in the inquiry to use them similarly. This method certainly increases the reliability of case-finding, but a questionnaire technique has many shortcomings. The number of questions limits the range of inquiry, so that some aspects of pathology will be missed if there are no questions to tap them. The rigidity of the prescribed question, a factor deliberately introduced in order to increase reliability, prevents the kind of informal cross-examination which a clinician uses when making his judgement about the patient's state. Finally, when using a questionnaire, the presence or absence of a symptom is based only on the patient's response, and thus the advantage of the clinician's experience gained over years of contact with psychiatric patients and of his ability to take account of the latter's response-set while making his decision is not available. This often makes a questionnaire lose in validity what it gains in reliability.

A compromise between the clinical approach and the questionnaire approach is the structured interview schedule. This is similar to a questionnaire in providing a standard check list of symptoms and of questions designed to elicit these symptoms, but differs from the latter in that a cross-examination is permitted to clarify doubts and in that the decision about the presence or absence of psychopathology is made by the investigator, guided by a set of standard definitions for the various symptoms. The structured interview technique therefore retains the flexibility of a clinical approach but it is more reliable because of the use of standard questions and definitions.

The measurement of psychiatric needs

It must be realised that both a questionnaire and a structured interview schedule, reliable as they are, do nothing more than ascertain the presence or absence of psychiatric symptoms, and symptoms on their own do not make a person a psychiatric case if by 'case' we mean someone who needs help and treatment. Surveys designed to ascertain the prevalence of symptoms have often shown more than half the population to be manifesting some sort of psychological disturbance. It is difficult to accept, however, that more than half the population is in need of psychiatric help! To determine this need it is necessary to measure certain other parameters besides the presence of psychiatric symptoms.

'Need for help' is not a unitary concept. It may be felt by the individual, his family, his neighbours or by the society at large. The person himself, those around him and the society may agree or disagree about the presence and degree of need. Healers, priests and law enforcers in a given community may view the need differently from each other and from those who complain.

Need is related to, but not the same thing as, *demand*. The demand for psychiatric help may be suppressed because of fear, shame, ignorance or a sense of hopelessness. On the other hand there may be an over-demand because of propaganda or fashion, as one suspects has been the case in certain strata of society in the U.S.A.

Need is related to, but not the same thing as, *morbidity* if by the latter term we mean a clinically recognisable pathology. A clinical abnormality may not require help if it is not sufficiently distressful or does not interfere with day-to-day functioning. On the other hand, a person may be extremely distressed even though his condition does not fall into any of the diagnostic categories recognised in current clinical jargon.

In the medical model this problem of the subjective element in recognition of need is side-stepped through the use of the concept of a 'clinically defined need' which is assumed to be present wherever a clinically recognisable 'disease entity' is identified. Inherent in this assumption is the belief that the person who has the disease needs help and that if he does not himself experience this need now, he will do so in future. These diseases are entities recognised by standard signs and symptoms and often confirmed through laboratory tests.

Unfortunately the disease concept can be applied to only a few of the conditions considered to be in the realm of a psychiatrist. Most psychiatric symptoms fail to coalesce into indisputable syndromes with a predictable progress. Under these circumstances one has to fall back on the first order value judgements concerning the person's need for treatment, about which there may or may not be agreement between the individual, his family, the doctor, the priest, the law enforcer and the society at large. Whose value judgement should be accepted? What criterion is the most appropriate for measuring psychiatric need?

There is a suggestion from some quarters that need should be assessed according to the treatment available. Mathew (1971) says that a need for medical care exists if an individual has an illness or disability for which an effective or acceptable treatment exists. This definition would apply to only a few psychiatric conditions and to even fewer if the criterion for effectiveness of treatment is of the order of that provided by antibiotics for infections. Psychiatry is a young science with a plethora of treatment philosophies and aims. According to some psychiatrists relief of symptoms is a sufficient criterion for effectiveness of treatment, while according to others nothing short of a complete personality change is sufficient. Whose criterion of effectiveness of treatment should be accepted?

Further, it is difficult to accept that a need for help disappears if an effective treatment is not available at the present stage of our knowledge. To take an analogy, does the need for food disappear if there is no food? Surely the availability of food is dependent on a host of factors which have nothing to do with the need for it.

So great are the difficulties in choosing the criteria for a measure of psychiatric need in the general population that until recently epidemiologists have been wary of attempting so formidable a task. There have, however, been two famous psychiatric surveys in which such an assessment was carried out, albeit crudely and, in our opinion, on the wrong lines.

In the Stirling County study (Leighton *et al.*, 1963) the first step was a symptom prevalence survey carried out by lay investigators. The judgement about the presence or absence of symptoms, however, was made by a board of trained psychiatrists who reviewed the protocols prepared by the field workers. Not only did these psychiatrists decide the presence or absence of symptoms; they also gave an A, B, C, D rating, the rating A being given to a person who, in their opinion, had an 80 per cent or more chance of being declared a psychiatric case, were he to be given a thorough psychiatric examination. B, C and D ratings represented progressively lesser confidence of this happening. Apart from the A, B, C, D rating a 'severity of impairment' rating was also given, on the basis of admittedly meagre information and from rather subjective impressions gained about the total life experience of the individual. The two kinds of ratings were combined in a purely arbitrary fashion to produce a typology. There were five types. Those belonging to type I were considered to be in the greatest need of psychiatric attention, and so on down the scale. The Stirling County study, pioneering work as it was, can be criticised on many grounds. The criticisms pertinent to the present discussion are as follows:

(a) The degree of need was decided, not by the sufferers, nor by the field investigators, but by psychiatrists who had had no direct contact with the respondents in the survey.

(b) The decisions about degrees of need were made on meagre information and the criteria for making such decisions were not made explicit.

(c) The final typology was created in a most arbitrary fashion, the logic of which was not clearly stated.

(d) Impairment over the whole life-span was estimated to decide the degree of present need for help: but judgements about events remote in time are notoriously unreliable.

In the Midtown Manhattan survey (Srole et al., 1962) respondents were categorised into five groups—from 'well' to 'incapacitated'—on information reporting both current symptoms and the 'total life pattern' of the individuals interviewed. All the criticisms applied to the Stirling County study apply to this survey also. There is an additional point to make: some symptoms were categorised as serious, others as moderate and still others as mild in their own right, without taking into consideration how distressful they were in a particular case. To categorise anxiety as more serious than earache, for example, seems too arbitrary a judgement.

To summarise, cross-cultural comparisons have a great potential for determining the relative significance of environmental factors in the development of mental disorder. However, researchers engaged in such comparisons face two major problems: that of establishing comparable definitions of psychiatric symptoms across cultures and the lack of suitable techniques for measuring the relevant socio-cultural parameters. They also share with psychiatric epidemiologists in general the difficulty of developing a reliable and valid method of defining a case in a non-referred population and of separating those in greater need of attention from the others. It was against this background that the Kota study was designed.

2

THE KOTA STUDY

The aim of the study was to compare the prevalence and patterns of mental disorder in three South Indian communities which, in spite of sharing the same environment, the same religion and the same language for centuries, have been able to maintain some easily perceptible differences in their way of life and cultural traditions.

The inquiry was carried out in a coastal village named Kota, situated in the South Kanara district of Karnataka State. The three communities were respectively the *Brahmins*, the *Bants* and the *Mogers*. The Brahmins and Bants are agriculturists ,while the Mogers are the local fishermen. The three groups differ in their socio-economic status, their food habits, their patterns of worship and the rigidity of their customs and taboos. The most striking difference, however—the one in fact which prompted our choice of these particular communities for this comparative study—is in their pattern of inheritance.

The Brahmins are patrilineal, that is to say, property is inherited through the male line from fathers to sons. The Bants and Mogers are matrilineal, property passing through the female line from maternal uncles to nephews. The matrilineal system has some interesting socio-cultural implications. The woman after marriage continues to reside in her own mother's house, visiting her husband's house for a few months in the year. Her children are brought up by their maternal uncles and have very little emotional attachment to their father.

We planned in our study to describe the socio-cultural differences observed in the three groups and to seek relationships between these cultural features and any differences in the prevalence of mental disorder revealed by our survey. In the previous chapter we have outlined the major methodological problems any such study must anticipate. Here we explain the steps taken to overcome some of these problems.

Selection of cultural groups for comparison

Cultural differences are, of course, best highlighted when vastly different nations are compared; however, as explained earlier, international comparisons of mental disorder are often of doubtful

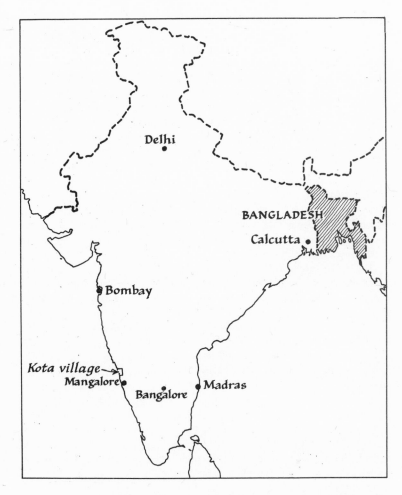

Map of India showing the location of Kota village.

validity because culturally dissimilar societies are likely to differ not only on several unmeasurable parameters but also in their very concept of mental disorder. The first step we took towards planning a methodologically sound cross-cultural study was to aim for *intra-national* rather than international comparisons. We looked for groups which would generally be similar except on a few important and measurable parameters. The fact that the three communities of Kota shared the same village, the same religion, the same language and the same health facilities made much easier the subsequent task of considering the effect of certain identifiable differences between them.

The detection of mental disorder

In the previous chapter we have stressed that the best method of obtaining a true prevalence of mental disorder is to conduct a population survey. We have also pointed out the defects in surveys based on clinical assessment and in those carried out using standard questionnaires.

In the Kota study we decided to compare the prevalence of mental disorder in the three communities, through a population survey using a 'structured interview' technique. As mentioned earlier this technique increases the flexibility of the interview without necessarily reducing its reliability.

On scrutinising several structured interview schedules developed to date we found them to be suffering from the following short-comings:

1. Most schedules are too long and time-consuming to be useful in a door-to-door survey where economy of time and effort is as important as the depth and range of inquiry. Goldberg and his colleagues recommend a two-stage procedure with a quick initial screening followed by a more detailed examination of the suspected cases in a realistic clinical setting (Goldberg *et al.*, 1970). This approach is certainly more economical, but those involved in field research are painfully aware of the difficulties entailed in contacting a respondent more than once. It is even more difficult to persuade people (who, it must be remembered, did not ask for the first interview nor sought help in the first instance) to come for another interview in a clinical setting. In the Indian rural scene where the people are not sophisticated enough to realise the long-range advantages of research, such an approach was unlikely to succeed.

2. It is well known that those suffering from psychiatric disorder may either be reluctant to divulge their symptoms because of social stigma or deny their presence because of poor insight. Con-

sequently, a clinician almost always tries to supplement the information gained from a patient with that obtained from a relative or a friend who has been in close contact with the patient. None of the structured interview schedules we examined was designed to obtain this extra information.

3. Perhaps the most unfortunate feature was that the schedules were without exception developed in the West and did not pay sufficient attention to the psychiatric problems common in an Indian setting, such as the phenomenon of spirit-possession, preoccupation with symptoms of sexual inadequacy, and the frequency of vague somatic symptoms of psychological origin.

In the Kota study we decided to construct a new structured interview schedule which would be free from the above defects. Our attempts led to the development of the 'Indian Psychiatric Interview Schedule' (IPIS) and the 'Indian Psychiatric Survey Schedule' (IPSS). A detailed account of the research involved in their construction and testing of their reliability has been published elsewhere (Kapur, Kapur and Carstairs, 1974, a and b) and this is also summarised in Chapter 7. It will be sufficient to mention here that the IPSS, which was used for the field survey in Kota, is an instrument designed to investigate the presence or absence of 125 psychiatric symptoms, with a special emphasis on those commonly encountered in an Indian setting. The schedule includes provision for an interview with a close relative. The inquiry proceeds through a multi-stage procedure, not all the stages being necessary for each respondent. A large part of the inquiry can be conducted by a non-psychiatrist. The procedure of the inquiry, the definition of symptoms and the criteria for deciding when a close relative is to be interviewed, are all fully standardised. The IPSS inquires about symptoms only; no attempt is made to combine the symptoms into psychiatric syndromes. The inadequacies of current psychiatric classification are such that we decided to forego such an attempt.

Measurement of psychiatric need

The IPSS simply ascertains the presence or absence of symptoms; but symptoms on their own do not make a person a psychiatric 'case' if by the latter term we mean someone who needs help or treatment. In the previous chapter we have explored the difficulties involved in obtaining a consensus as to what constitutes psychiatric need. We have also given an account of two famous studies in which rather imperfect attempts were made to formulate objective assessments of this need.

In the Kota study we planned to approach the issue from three directions. A 'need' was defined to be present if the subject had one or more symptoms, and had either:

(a) consulted any of the agencies serving the function of a healer in the local context. These agencies included the practitioner of Western medicine, the practitioner of Indian medicine, the astrologer, the Shaman (locally called the *Patri*) and the temple priest.

(b) declared during the interview an inability to cope with his day-to-day work and social relations, irrespective of whether he had consulted anyone or not.

(c) shown, on objective examination, a decline in his day-to-day functioning. It proved very difficult to decide the criterion against which the individual's social functioning was to be measured. One thing seemed certain: the criterion must derive from the norms of the group to which the person belonged and not from the aspirations and objectives of the investigator. With this in view, a social functioning questionnaire suitable for the Kota population was developed for the purposes of the study.

The socio-cultural correlates

Since the main aim of the study was to seek an explanation for differences in the prevalence of mental disorder in the three communities, in terms of the socio-cultural differences observed in these communities, it was necessary to explore the latter in some detail. The following studies were carried out to gather the relevant information:

(a) A preliminary survey of the whole village, to collect quantitative information about some selected socio-cultural variables.

(b) A study of the village people, especially those belonging to the three communities, on a participant-observation model.

(c) A study of attitudes towards modernisation in the three communities.

(d) A measure of each community's members' self-reported 'social distance' from other groups.

(e) A study of local healers and their clientele.

(f) A study of community attitudes towards making use of different types of healers.

The specific aims of the study

These were as follows:

1. To examine whether there were significant differences in the prevalence of psychiatric symptoms amongst the Brahmins, Bants and Mogers, and to explore the nature of any such differences.

2. To see whether the rate of prevalence of symptoms was related to demographic and socio-cultural variables such as age, sex, income,

occupation, marital status, family organisation and parental death during childhood.

3. To see whether differences in the prevalence of symptoms were related to the different residence patterns found in the patrilineal and matrilineal groups.

4. To see whether differences in the prevalence of symptoms were related to differential exposure to social change. Among the various indicators of social change, changes in residence pattern shown by formerly matrilineal families were chosen for particular examination. We decided to investigate whether the prevalence of symptoms was different in those who normally lived apart from their spouse, in accordance with the traditional matrilineal pattern, and in those who now lived continuously with their spouse.

5. To study respondents' patterns of consultation and to see whether these were related to socio-cultural factors.

6. To examine the relationship between the number and types of symptoms reported, and the other indicators of psychiatric need.

7. To see whether the levels of psychiatric 'need' were different in the three communities.

The operational procedure

The study was planned in Edinburgh during 1968–1969. In October 1969 we were fortunate enough to obtain a financial grant from the Foundations Fund for Research in Psychiatry in support of the project. In February 1970, Dr Kapur left for India and his first task was to establish two bases of operation: one at the All-India Institute of Mental Health, Bangalore, and the other at Kasturba Medical College, Manipal. The development of the interview schedule was carried out at Bangalore, while the socio-anthropological investigations as well as the field survey were launched from Manipal, a town in the heart of the South Kanara district. Kota was chosen as the village for study since it was readily accessible from Manipal (only 18 miles away) and had large enough populations belonging to the three communities to satisfy our statistical requirements. The field work was completed in about $2\frac{1}{2}$ years. The following are some important landmarks of the field work:

1. The preliminary survey of the village and the collection of the socio-demographic data was carried out in August–October 1970.

2. The participant-observation study was carried out between November 1970 and November 1971.

3. The studies on community attitudes as well as the preparation of the social functioning questionnaire were carried out between November 1971 and June 1972.

4. The preparation and standardisation of the IPIS and IPSS were carried out at the All-India Institute of Mental Health and the associated mental hospital between June 1970 and June 1972.

5. The field survey of mental disorder amongst the three communities was carried out during July–October 1972.

6. The analysis of the results was carried out at Edinburgh University during 1973.

The whole field operation was directly planned and supervised by Dr Kapur who also carried out the analysis of the survey data in Edinburgh during 1973. During the field work he maintained constant consultation with Dr Carstairs through correspondence. Dr Carstairs came to the field area twice during the course of the study to review progress and to help in planning the next stages of the inquiry.*

The plan of this book

In reporting a multifaceted study such as this, we are aware that we are addressing ourselves to at least two audiences: to those who share our particular research interests, and to the much wider public who are concerned with the quality of life in the developing countries. The former may be as interested in the technical details of our research methods as in our findings; for their benefit, and for our own satisfaction, we are publishing a series of research reports in the appropriate scientific journals. In this book, however, we have deliberately omitted many of the technical details and have tried instead to give a coherent account, in narrative form, of the communities we studied, the stages of our inquiry, our major findings, and the conclusions which we derived from them.

In the next two chapters we describe the salient features of the Kota village community as a whole and, in greater detail, the characteristics of the three sub-groups which were the subject of our household survey. We then devote one chapter to a description

* A number of other persons contributed to different stages of the field work, as follows:

The socio-anthropological investigations were carried out mainly by Mr K. N. K. Eshwar, a sociologist, with the assistance of Mr Guruva Markala, a local guide. In the later part of these investigations Mr Eshwar was assisted by Miss Kshama, a psychiatric social worker, and Miss Lalitha, a sociologist.

Mrs Malavika Kapur, a clinical psychologist, played a major part in the development of the psychiatric interview schedules. She was assisted during the reliability studies by two psychiatrists, Dr S. M. Channabasavana and Dr Sayeed Ahmed. Dr Sayeed Ahmed was the leader of the team which conducted the door-to-door survey. Mr Eshwar, Miss Kshama, Miss Lalitha and Mr Guruva Markala were the other members of this team.

the different types of healers to whom the villagers have recourse from time to time. The following three Chapters (6–8) give an account of the preparation, conduct and findings of our survey of psychiatric symptoms, followed in Chapters 9–11 by a consideration of the social correlates of symptoms, the degree to which they are disabling and the patterns of help-seeking. In Chapter 12 we discuss, in the light of our findings, a possible measure of the extent of need for the relief of psychiatric symptoms, in this community. In the final chapter we consider the wider implications of our findings, and indicate the feasibility of a low-cost public health programme which could provide some basic mental health care in areas of the developing countries where no such facilities yet exist.

3

KOTA AND ITS PEOPLE

The village

Though often referred to as a village, Kota is a *Panchayat*, an administrative unit comprising three small villages, Giliyar, Kota-thettu and Manoor, and having a population of roughly 9000 persons. It belongs to the district South Kanara, which lies on the west coast of India, halfway between Bombay and Cape Comorin, occupying a narrow strip of land between the Western Ghats and the Arabian Sea. The district, which forms a part of Karnataka state, is 150 miles in length and on average 25 miles broad. According to popular mythology this mass of land was reclaimed from the sea by the demi-god Parasu-Rama along with another strip of land to the south, now the state of Kerala. As the story goes, Parasu-Rama stood on the highest cliff in the Western Ghats and threw his mighty axe into the Arabian Sea, which receded from the point where the axe fell, leaving a fertile shelf of land between the mountain range and the seashore.

In the northern and eastern parts of South Kanara are hilly tropical forests which form a rich source of timber. Here and there the forests have been cleared away and replaced by rubber, coffee and areca nut plantations. The western and southern parts are flat and largely cultivated. The long coastal belt is lined with coconut groves and has some of the most exquisite palm-fringed sandy beaches in the country. Kota lies in this coastal belt.

The weather in the district is warm and humid throughout the year except for a short cool season during December and January — not really a winter, the temperature hardly ever falling below 20°C. The forests, the plantations and the agriculture are all nourished by the monsoon rains which give rise to small rainwater rivulets — there are no perennial rivers. On the average it rains about 125–150 inches a year, almost all of the rainfall being in the months of June to September. The sandy soil is unable to retain the water and the country, which is lush green during the monsoon season, rapidly becomes brown by January and dusty brown by April.

Till recently, because of the steep Western Ghats, communication with the rest of the state was rather poor. There are excellent roads

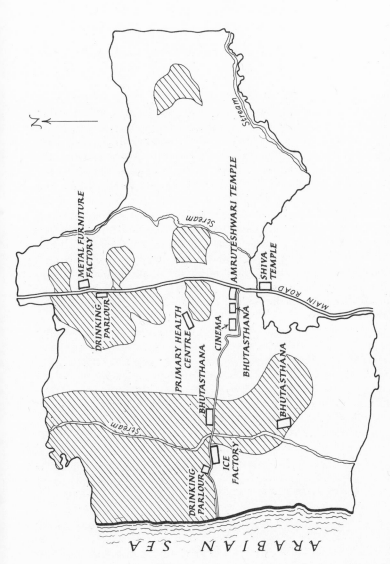

Kota village. *The shaded sections represent the areas in which the interviews were carried out. Housing is relatively dense on either side of the main road running through the village; elsewhere houses are scattered throughout the area.*

now and a railway line is under construction between Hassan, a town on the plateau on the eastern side of the Ghats, and Mangalore, the capital city of South Kanara. The Bombay–Mangalore highway passes through Kota, as a result of which its inhabitants have easy access to all the major towns on the whole length of the West coast. Mangalore is about 70 miles away to the South, and Goa some 250 miles to the North.

Kannada is the official language of Karnataka state. In South Kanara, however, Kannada is spoken only in the smaller northern region, while in the larger southern region the language is Tulu, which is distinct enough from Kannada not to be considered a dialect of the latter. Kota lies in the Kannada-speaking region.

By Indian standards, Kota is a modern village as far as its civic and technical amenities are concerned. It is fully electrified and has a post and telegraph office, two banks, a government health centre, two private practitioners of Western medicine, a cinema hall, six schools, an ice factory and another small factory making steel furniture. Excellent bus and taxi services connect Kota with the surrounding areas. Private run 'tourist' taxis are a feature of South Kanara, the drivers often accomplishing the astonishing feat of carrying 9–10 passengers in modest-sized vehicles. Even the poor take advantage of the bus and taxi services. Bullock carts are widely used, but mainly for carrying merchandise and hardly ever for human transportation.

The portion of the highway which passes through Kota is called the 'town' by the villagers. It is in the 'town' that the major business is conducted, and it is there that one goes to relax in the evenings. Besides the post office, the doctors and the two banks mentioned above, the 'town' has many grocery and general merchandise shops, goldsmiths, blacksmiths, carpenters, two temples, two liquor parlours, the Panchayat office, a chemist and the houses belonging to the richer section of the village. The only cinema hall in the village, which began to operate in 1970, is just off the main road.

Although communications with the outside world are very good, those within the village are rather poor. There is one jeepable road to the sea-front where cars can be used with some difficulty. To reach any other place in the 15 square mile Panchayat area it is very difficult to use any vehicle, even a bicycle.

The single most important contributing factor to the poor communications is the village housing pattern. In the majority of Indian villages the houses and huts are clustered together in a confined space with the fields stretching all around. Kota, however, in conformity with the pattern prevailing on the west coast, has a scattered housing pattern. Each landlord builds his house in the middle of his fields, and near each landlord's house are two or three huts belonging to the tenants and labourers attached to the land. To go from one house to another one has to cross the fields, or at best there may be a narrow footpath between two fields. One cannot easily shout across to one's neighbour as one can in a village of the clustered type; nor is it easy to assemble after work in some central place. In a clustered village one invariably finds a meeting-place where the villagers collect to sit and gossip after the day's work is over. There is no such place in Kota. This does not mean that Kota people do not gossip. The legendary grape-vine is as well spread here as anywhere else! Villagers do go to the 'town' in the evenings but it is not easy to reach in the dark, especially in the rainy season.

Most houses belonging to the poor people in the village are little more than a space enclosed by dried palm-leaf walls, roofed by a thatch of paddy straw. The houses of the better-off are made of bricks and have slanting tiled roofs. They usually all follow the same architectural pattern, and what distinguishes a richer from a poorer man's house is its size.

One enters a typical Kota house through a large compound enclosed by walls made of brick or mud. In the centre of the courtyard stands the sacred Tulsi (basil) plant, and in a corner one can see a grain store made of knitted sheaves of straw containing the rice crop of the season. One enters the main house through a verandah (a raised covered platform) and this is where the visitors are welcomed. The living space usually consists of a rectangular raised platform surrounding a central courtyard. Here the family lives and sleeps. There may be one or two rooms but they are used more for storing household articles than for living. There may be a room or a corner for the deity. Beyond the living space is the kitchen and the dining-hall. The larger the dining-hall the richer the family is presumed to be, the size of the hall reflecting the number of people who can be invited and accommodated on feast days. Behind the house proper is the bathroom and the well. There is usually no lavatory, the villagers preferring to go to the fields for defaecation. What is most striking about the housing is the absence of privacy. The members of the household, even young couples, share the same living space and sleep in the same area, though the newly married show great ingenuity in finding corners away from the others.

A feature of Kota which it shares with other coastal villages is its cleanliness. The stench of open drains, so frequently encountered in villages of northern India, is absent. Everyone—even the poorest— takes a bath at least once a day. Even if there is only one change of clothes, the clothes are washed daily.

Another feature which would strike a visitor from northern India is the absence of any Purdah system amongst the women. Influenced by Muslim tradition, northern women veil their faces in the presence of strangers and of the male members of the family who are older than their husbands. In Kota one sees gaily dressed women with flowers in their hair greeting and talking to visitors without inhibition. This should not make one jump to the conclusion that women here enjoy a higher social status than do their sisters in the north — far from it. The matter will be discussed later in greater detail.

Religion and caste groups

Kota has a small Muslim and an even smaller Christian community. All the rest are Hindus belonging to several caste groups. The principal caste groups can be categorised as follows:

1. BRAHMINS: Further divided into Kota Brahmins, Goud Saraswats, Shivalli Brahmins and Sthanik Brahmins. Brahmins are ritually the highest group and are mainly landowners. Most school teachers are Kota Brahmins and most Goud Saraswats are involved in trade.

2. BANTS: Traditionally soldiers but now mainly agriculturists.

3. MOGERS: The fishermen caste.

4. BHILLAVAS: Traditionally toddy-tappers but now mainly involved in agricultural labour.

5. DEVADIGAS: Traditionally musicians but now mainly involved in agricultural labour.

6. JOGIS: Traditionally bangle makers. Now mainly sellers of factory-produced bangles, or agricultural labourers.

7. ACHARIS and GANIGAS: Traditionally skilled craftsmen. Even nowadays usually involved in the trades of carpenter, goldsmith, silversmith, blacksmith, etc.

8. MADIVALAS: Washermen.

9. SHETTIGARS: Weavers.

10. BHANDARIS: Barbers.

11. HOLEYAS: Traditionally untouchables; now mainly involved in agricultural labour and providing essential civic services.

Caste and the concept of pollution

According to traditional beliefs any contact between a member of a 'higher' caste and that of a 'lower' caste resulted in a ritual pollution of the former. The contact might be through touch, inter-dining or sex. In certain parts of the country the concept of a defiling contact was elaborated to include being in the same room or even

walking along the same road. The complexity of the purificatory
rite or penance one had to undergo in order to get rid of the pollution increased in proportion to the 'distance' between the two castes
involved. In the extreme case the 'polluted' individual might find
himself excommunicated by his caste-fellows.

There is evidence that pollution rules were strictly observed in
Kota as recently as thirty years ago, not only between higher and
lower castes but also between sub-categories of the Untouchables.
The rules are much more relaxed now, and caste barriers are
breaking down. During the study period we did not hear of any
purificatory rite or excommunication. We found different caste
members sitting in the same cinema hall and eating in the same
restaurants. However, intermarriage between different castes is still
prohibited. Members of higher castes will not eat food cooked by
members of the lower castes. Though prohibited by law, untouch-
ability is still practised to a large extent. Educated Brahmins criticise
the caste system and send their children to the same school as other
castes. However, the association seems limited to the schoolroom;
we hardly ever noticed the children from families of different castes
playing together after school hours, even though their parents were
neighbours and shared the same socio-economic and educational
background.

About half of the caste groups in Kota follow the patrilineal joint
family pattern, while the other half follow a variation of the matrilineal system, known locally as Aliya-Santana.

The patrilineal joint family

Amongst the local patrilineal groups, ancestral property is passed
from the males of one generation to all male offspring of the next
generation and not only to the eldest son, as in some patrilineal
societies. The male members of the various generations live in the
same house along with their wives and children.

Any male adult can ask for his share of land and separate out
with his wife and children. This happens not infrequently, with the
advantage that the size of the joint family is kept within reasonable
proportions, but the disadvantage is that the land is broken into
smaller and smaller pieces. Occasionally an individual might sell
his share of land to the other members of his family and leave the
village with his wife and children to seek his fortune elsewhere.

While some people have always left the fold of the joint family in
the fashion described above, this has been happening much more
frequently in recent years. This is partly due to the rapid industrialisation in the country and to the promise of a more com-

fortable life in the cities. It is also due to a basic change in attitudes: the desire to copy city life where the nuclear family is necessarily more common, the impact of the Western way of life through school education, the influence of books and films which often highlight the interpersonal problems in joint families, have all helped to reduce the stigma and shame which used to be associated with the break-up of a joint family. Quarrels between brothers, and the tensions between a young wife and her mother-in-law or her un-married sisters-in-law which used to be swept under the carpet to keep the illusion of a united family, take their toll much more easily now. Even when the older members want to keep the family to-gether they find that their authority is no longer unquestionable, as used to be the case: their voice cannot override the arguments of the more educated and more daring present-day youngsters as ruthlessly as used to be the rule.

The Aliya-Santana system

Translated literally, Aliya-Santana means 'nephew-child'. Ac-cording to this system, the ancestral property is vested in the female lineage, but in practice it passes from the maternal uncle to his sister's son. Management of the property is done by men only. Ac-cording to legend this system was started by the King Bhutala Pandya. As the story goes, he was once cursed and was told that the curse could be removed only by his sacrificing one of his children. The children refused this honour but one of his sister's children offered himself for the sacrifice. At this time the king decreed that in future amongst the people of his kingdom all property would be inherited by the children of a deceased man's sister and not by his own children.

Whatever the origins of the system, it has interesting social im-plications. On marriage, the wife does not move into her husband's house as happens in a patrilineal society; nor, as in a matrilocal system, does the man move into his wife's house. Traditionally the man continues to live in his ancestral home, his wife alternately spending six months with him and six months in her father's house. The amount of time spent by the wife with her husband has, how-ever, always been subject to great variation. The upkeep of the children and the decision about their marriage, etc. are the re-sponsibility of the wife's brother. When young, they accompany their mother when she goes to live with her husband, but as they grow older they see less and less of their father, staying at home to work on the family land under the direction of their maternal uncles.

This system is quite similar to the one practised in Kerala state before 1912 when the king of Trivandrum passed a law making matrilineal inheritance illegal. The king of Cochin, the neighbouring state, passed a similar law in 1920, and the British Government of Madras presidency followed suit in 1935 making Aliya-Santana inheritance illegal in the coastal area under their occupation. This included the South Kanara district.

The impact of the law was much weaker in the British region than in the princely states of Trivandrum and Cochin where, according to the historian V. Iyer, 34,000 clans partitioned their property within five years of enactment of the new laws. This was presumably because of the British Government's policy not to interfere with native cultural traditions so long as they did not obstruct the processes of government. As a result, even after Independence, the majority of matrilineal caste groups of South Kanara continued to practise their traditional inheritance pattern.

In 1957 the National Government of India passed the Hindu Code Bill which made matrilineal inheritance illegal in all parts of India. This law was enforced more strictly, and as a result the Aliya-Santana caste groups in South Kanara are now in a state of transition. The consequent changes in residence pattern are far from complete, and in our survey we observed the following variations:

1. Change to patrilineal inheritance as well as to the residence pattern of a patrilineal family.

2. Change to the patrilineal inheritance but no change in residence pattern.

3. One or more male members have changed over to the patrilineal residence pattern and have their wives and children living with them. However, one or more of their sisters have husbands who still do not observe the new living arrangement. The family now has to support not only the sisters and their children but also the brothers' wives and children. This results in economic hardship for the men of the family; but also it inevitably creates tension between the sisters-in-law and their children, who vie with each other for rights and status.

4. Occasionally the wife wins the status struggle, and her husband's sister is no longer made welcome in the house. However, she is also not welcome in her husband's house since his family still follows the traditional pattern. This is a great source of stress to the sister and her children.

5. Occasionally the husband of the woman unwelcome in both quarters takes the initiative and builds a separate hut for her and

the children; but more often than not he himself does not have the courage to go and live with them! This leads to the very awkward situation of women and children being obliged to live on their own while their husbands and brothers are still alive and in the same village.

6. Some couples have the courage to break away from the confusion and start a nuclear family.

As can be seen, this transition phase can give rise to stress, especially to women and children. The women are insecure while the children look for an identifiable father figure. The new opportunities for education have brought further problems to these unhappy children. Their maternal uncles are wary of accepting new responsibilities, while their fathers still tend to think that it is the uncles' duty to pay for their education.

One would think that a quick way out would be to hasten the process of transition, but it is not easy to change the way of life and to forego rights to what one considers to be one's own property. Further, most of the members of older generations (and many among the new generation) are afraid that a break from tradition would provoke the wrath of the gods and spirits who control their destiny.

The means of livelihood

The economy of Kota rests mainly on agriculture and fishing. This is supplemented to a certain extent by the money sent by those who left Kota to work in the big cities. A few are involved in trade, and a much smaller number in toddy tapping and service occupations.

Agriculture

Kota soil is sandy and generally of poor quality. It is traditionally divided into *wet land* and *dry land*. The former is irrigated to varying extent and is used for farming. The latter is used for grazing and as a source of firewood. There are three types of wet land:

(a) irrigated during the rains only;

(b) irrigated from rainwater collected in ponds and hence available throughout the year;

(c) flooded during the rains and hence rendered useless for almost half the year, yielding a crop after the floods recede.

About one-third of the wet land belongs to the third category. A small proportion (less than one-sixth) belongs to the second category.

Paddy is the main crop. There are three kinds of paddy crop:

'Kathe' before the rains, 'Suggi' after the rains, and 'Kolke' (on the best irrigated lands) before the spring. It is possible to grow two crops of lentils between or instead of the paddy crops. The majority of the farmers grow one crop of paddy and another of lentils. Some enterprising farmers (less than 10 per cent) manage to grow a third crop.

With the help of electric pumps (which are expensive and which only a few can afford) a little less than 5 per cent of the cultivable land has been converted into coconut gardens. It takes about ten years for a coconut tree to start yielding fruit, but once it becomes functional, land on which coconuts are grown brings in at least three times the income provided by paddy cultivation.

The ploughing is done by a wooden plough drawn by buffaloes. Modern fertilisers and modern seeds are used by very few. The traditional fertiliser is a natural manure prepared from green leaves spread in the cowshed where they become mixed with cattle dung and urine. It is apparent that Kota has not yet been affected by the 'green revolution' spreading in other parts of India.

Not all the land is tilled by the owners. Part is tilled by tenant-cultivators (sharecroppers) and by hired agricultural labour.

On the average an acre of land in Kota yields 800–1200 kilogrammes of paddy per year. The tenants have to give about 150–200 kilogrammes per acre to the owner. However, this is done only once a year—any extra crop during the year going wholly to the tenant.

The agricultural labourers are employed in special operations such as ploughing, sowing, transplanting and harvesting. The average landless labourer is employed for between four and six months a year. The labourers are paid their daily wages in rice— 2 kilogrammes per working day for men and $1\frac{1}{2}$ kilogrammes for a woman.

Fishing

The most common traditional form of fishing is 'Mari-Bale', or long line fishing, where one end of a long fishing net is taken into the sea by a boat, the other being held on the shore by a group of fishermen. The net is drawn in to the shore after four or five hours. The operation is generally carried out once a day during the dry season but sometimes twice a day if the conditions permit.

One Mari-Bale unit is manned by about 100 fishermen who all own a share in the equipment costing about Rs 50,000. Mari-Bale is well organised with a leader called 'Thandela', an accountant called 'Shanbhog' and four assistant leaders called 'Gurikaras'. The leaders see to it that the catch is equally divided amongst the Bale members. In a good season a fisherman can earn about Rs 1000. There are four Mari-Bale groups in Kota but some of their members are from surrounding villages.

There are other traditional forms of fishing. One is the off-season 'Kai Rampani' which employs small rowing boats. Another is the rarely used deep-sea long line fishing. There are also two 'Patte Bales', or sail-boat fishing teams, which work from January to August and carry out deep-sea fishing.

These three types of traditional fishing are not competitive with Mari-Bale but only supplement its catch. The real competition comes from modern mechanised fishing. The first mechanised boat appeared about twenty years ago but the real impetus has come from a recent state-supported Agricultural Re-finance Corporation. This corporation, the ARC as it is commonly called, offers loans on easy terms so that a newly-purchased boat can be fully owned by a five-man crew in roughly six to eight years. The ARC also runs a fishery school.

The take-home earnings of a mechanised boat worker are only about Rs 750 per year but his income is much more stable than that of a Mari-Bale fisherman.

Until recently the fish was sold locally or dried and sent out. Now there is an iceplant in nearby Manoor and frozen fish is exported. There has been a sudden spurt in the canning industry in Mangalore which has much improved the lot of the fishermen.

Toddy tapping

This is the caste occupation of the Bhillava community and practised solely by them. The toddy is tapped from the coconut or palmyra palms in bottles or pots attached to cuts made on the stem near the top of the tree. A tapper can earn about Rs 800–1000 a year. Not many Bhillavas of Kota are involved in this occupation, because there are not many coconut or toddy-bearing trees in this area.

Trade

Most grocery and general merchandise shops are owned by Brahmins of the Goud Saraswat sub-caste. A small trader earns on the average Rs 2000–3000 a year. The few wholesale fish merchants earn about Rs 5000–10,000 a year. One Bant family owns a factory producing steel articles of furniture. There are a few itinerant merchants who travel from place to place and sell their wares in the weekly markets.

Restaurant enterprises

Kota Brahmins have been famous in southern and western India for more than fifty years. They work in restaurants specialising in local and South Indian dishes, which have come to be known as 'Udipi restaurants', taking their name from the nearby town of Udipi; these restaurants can now be found in cities in almost every part of India. This tradition has now been taken up by other local communities also. Usually such people leave the village young, working as waiters in Bangalore, Bombay and other towns. Some of them work their way up until they own small restaurants themselves. Most of these émigrés send about half of their salary home to their families. The majority come back to Kota when they are old. The money sent by the émigrés and brought back by those who return is a great support to the local economy and has also been applied to the construction of several new schools and temples in the village.

Education facilities

Kota has six primary schools, two high schools, one junior college and one vocational training school. One school is run by the fishery department, three by the government education department, and the others by private bodies. The first school was established in the year 1900 and the latest one (the junior college) only in 1970.

Education is free up to the primary level, after which a nominal fee of Rs 3 per year is charged. Most teachers are Kota Brahmins. The teachers are poorly paid and carry out their duties with rather poor library or audio-visual aids. Most education seems to consist of rote-learning, very little effort being made to stimulate the children's curiosity, imagination and creativity. It must be remembered, however, that South Kanara has one of the highest literacy rates in India. In Kota about 90 per cent of the children between the ages of 6–10 go to school.

The Panchayat

Local administration is carried out by the Panchayat board which is responsible for providing public works, civic amenities and money for special contingencies like floods, etc. The Panchayat gets its revenue by levying taxes on buildings and vehicles, and also gets a 30 per cent share of the land revenue.

Panchayat members are elected once in four years through a total suffrage with a secret ballot. There are 19 members on the Panchayat board. Anyone can stand for election but one seat is reserved for the previously oppressed communities and four for women.

Kota Brahmins hold the largest number of seats in the current Panchayat though their community is smaller than that of the Mogers or the Bhillavas who hold one seat each. The Bants have five seats though once again they are a relatively small community. It is apparent that mere numerical strength plays very little part in determining the power structure of the village.

The pattern of worship

Except for the Brahmins, who worship the major gods of the Hindu pantheon, most of the Kota villagers are primarily worshippers of lesser spirits, or *Bhutas*, whose names and attribtues of supernatural authority are recognised only within a restricted local area. It is not uncommon, however, to see non-Brahmins going to the temples of major Hindu deities, and Brahmins visiting the *Bhuta-sthanas* (spirit-shrines). Snake worship is also popular with all the villagers. There are innumerable temples, snake-shrines and spirit-shrines in Kota. In addition, most families have a corner reserved for the worship of their household god.

Amongst the temples, or *Devasthanas*, the most popular are those in the 'town' of which one is devoted to Vishnu (the creator), another to Shiva (the destroyer), and the third to the goddess Amruteshwari—an incarnation of Kali. At least one service of worship is held in each temple every day, and more services are held on festivals and special occasions. The priests in all the temples are Kota Brahmins, except for Amruteshwari whose priests belong to the Ganiga caste. There is a tradition of offering animal sacrifices to this goddess.

The Bhuta-sthanas vary in size from a small enclosure around a sacred stone to buildings as large as temples. Whereas one worships gods to seek favours or to sing their praises, the Bhutas are worshipped in order to prevent their causing harm. According to mythology, Shiva created an army of 1000 'Ganas' (Bhuta-servants) to punish the wicked. These Ganas can take the form of a man, a woman or an animal or that of some unearthly creature.

The most common form of Bhuta-worship is to give an offering of areca palm flowers accompanied by a prayer. A special form of worship is 'Kola' when the Bhuta-priest becomes possessed by the Bhuta and dances throughout the night. This is a costly affair usually organised and paid for by someone who has taken a vow.

About 50 miles from the Kota Panchayat area is a Bhuta-temple called Dharmasthala where one of the most powerful of the Bhutas resides. People from all over the district including those from Kota go there to get their wishes granted, to rid themselves of illness or affliction by minor Bhutas, or just to fulfil a vow.

The Christians and the Muslims have their own Church and mosque respectively.

A survey of the socio-demographic characteristics of Kota

In August 1970 a census was carried out in Kota to define the size of the village population, to prepare a village directory, and to collect some hard data on selected socio-demographic variables which would enable us to describe the community with some precision. The whole operation, which took about three months to complete, was carried out by two members of the team, a sociologist (K. N. K. Eshwar) and the village guide (Guruva Markala), under the direct supervision of Dr Kapur. They conducted a house-to-house survey and, with the help of a standard pre-coded questionnaire, collected the desired information about each household from one or more adult members present in the house at that moment.

A directory was prepared which identified each individual by his family code and his personal code and by an 'area of residence' code. This directory made it possible during the later stages of our research to locate any individual within a matter of minutes; it also facilitated the sampling procedure.

The following information about the village people was obtained in this survey:

Population

There were 9111 permanent residents in the village, a permanent resident being defined as one who had lived in the village for at least nine months during the preceding year. There were 3973 males and 5138 females. Table 3.1 gives the number of males and females in each religious and caste group.

The Mogers are the largest and the Christians the smallest group in the village. Women outnumber men in each group. This is attributable to selective emigration on the part of the men, many of whom leave the village to seek work elsewhere. Table 3.2 shows a 1:1 male-female ratio amongst those below 14 years of age. In the older groups the relative proportion of men falls considerably, rising once again in those above the age of 40, but not quite reaching equality with women. This late rise in the proportion of men appears to be due to the émigrés coming back home in their old age.

TABLE 3.1

Religion, caste and sex distribution in Kota village

Religion	Caste	Males	Females	Total	Percentage of total population
HINDUS	Kota Brahmins	617	814	1431	16
	Other Brahmins	442	535	977	11
	Ganigas and Acharis	315	388	703	8
	Bants	366	435	801	9
	Mogers	944	1208	2152	24
	Bhillavas	693	939	1632	18
	Devadigas	183	255	438	5
	Holeyas	150	205	355	4
	Other Hindus	64	75	139	1
MUSLIMS		155	208	363	4
CHRISTIANS		44	76	120	1
TOTAL		3973	5138	9111	

TABLE 3.2

Sex distribution in successive age groups

	Age groups				
	−14	15–20	21–40	41–60	61+
Males	49%	37%	38%	44%	43%
Females	51%	63%	62%	56%	57%
Number of persons	3927	1129	2244	1323	488

Occupational structure

An analysis was made of the occupations of men and women respectively in the different caste and religious groups. The analysis was limited to those aged 10 or above and excluded those claiming to be students, or unemployed, or retired from active work. In the case of men, if a person had more than one occupation he was assigned to the category in which he spent most of his time. Women were designated housewives only if they had no other occupation.

In summary it was found that amongst the men, the Kota Brahmins had the highest proportion of owner cultivators and of those employed in service occupations (including schoolteaching). 'Other Brahmins' showed the highest proportion of tradesmen. This is presumably because the majority in this category are Goud-Saraswats, trade and business being the traditional occupations of their sub-caste. While 62 per cent of the Acharis and Ganigas are engaged in their caste occupations as carpenters, goldsmiths and blacksmiths, only half of the Mogers and only 10 per cent of the Bhillavas are engaged in their respective caste occupations of fishing and toddy-tapping. Most of the Holeyas (the untouchables) are involved in agricultural labour. The Muslims and Christians do not have any caste occupations and are mainly skilled craftsmen, or businessmen, or employed in service.

A large majority of the Brahmin and Muslim women are housewives only, and do no other work. More than half of the Bhillava, Devadiga and Holeya women engage in agricultural labour, while only 13 per cent of the Brahmin women and 9 per cent of the Bant women work in the fields. Those are presumably landowning widows or women whose men are employed away from Kota.

Economic status

In order to permit comparison of the income-level of groups, with very different degrees of involvement in monetary transactions, a rough estimate was made of the per capita income, in rupees per annum, for the Kota population, which was then arbitrarily divided into three economic categories. In doing so, allowances were made for the type of land cultivated, for ownership or tenant status, and for the number of children under the age of 12.

A note was made of the total 'wet' land and garden land owned or cultivated under tenancy by each family in the village. Incomes derived from employment or shopkeeping by one or more members of the family, as well as monies received regularly from relatives or family members living outside the village, were also recorded. Fishermen's income was determined by making a rough estimate of the previous year's fish catch and sale in consultation with the Bali leaders.

Income from owned 'wet' land was assessed at Rs. 1000 per acre a year and that from garden land at Rs. 3000 a year. The income from a land cultivated on tenancy was assessed as Rs. 750 a year since part of the produce had to be given over to the land owner. These values were fixed in accordance with the opinions of the village leaders.

The yearly incomes derived from various sources were added up and divided by the total number of family members to derive the per capita income. For this purpose any one below the age of 12 years was taken as half a member.

No attempt was made to allot bonus points for growing more than two crops a year or for indulging in mechanised fishing. Also no deductions were made for expenses incurred in maintenance and improvement of land and boats. Such sophisticated calculations were considered beyond the scope of the present study. Our aim was primarily to conduct a comparative analysis, and we decided that the influence of these other variables would be evenly distributed among the three groups. Having totalled the number of rupees of annual income per head, households were assigned to one of three income-level categories.

(a) Those with per capita incomes of Rs. 200 a year or less: it appears that these people must be having great difficulty in meeting the minimum needs for food and clothing and were designated as living below subsistence level.

(b) Those with per capita incomes of between Rs. 201 and Rs. 800 a year: they appeared to be leading an average existence.

(c) Those with per capita incomes of more than Rs. 800 a year: they appeared to be comfortable compared to the village standards and were designated as living a 'comfortable existence'. Table 3.3 compares the different religious and caste groups on economic status.

TABLE 3.3

Relative economic status of religious and caste groups

Religion	Caste	No.	Percentage in three income groups		
			Below subsistence level %	Average %	Comfortable existence %
HINDUS	Kota Brahmins	1431	9	50	41
	Other Brahmins	977	13	54	33
	Ganigas and Acharis	703	33	33	33
	Bants	801	36	53	11
	Mogers	2152	24	69	7
	Bhillavas	1632	65	32	3
	Devadigas	438	70	10	20
	Holeyas	355	100	—	—
	Other Hindus	139	30	60	10
MUSLIMS		363	—	80	20
CHRISTIANS		120	40	40	20
TOTAL		9111	34	48	18

The Brahmins are the richest, with very few living below subsistence level and more than 40 per cent living at the 'comfortable' level. The Holeyas are the poorest, all of them living below subsistence level. This ranking was expected and serves to validate the index. A high proportion of the Bhillavas and Devadigas also live below subsistence level. None of the Muslims does so, but on the other hand, only 20 per cent of Muslims lead a 'comfortable' existence.

Education

In all, some 37 per cent of the villagers can read or write. The overall literacy rate is, however, a poor indication of the present-day trends since it includes in its denominator many old people who were not exposed to the current high evaluation of education and who, in their childhood days, would have had few opportunities of going to school even if they had so desired.

To examine the effect of recent trends it was decided to compare the proportions of children in the age group 6–10 years who were attending school at the time of inquiry in each of the main caste and religious groups. Table 3.4 gives the results. It shows that all the Christian boys and girls and a very high proportion of the Brahmin

TABLE 3.4

Proportion of school attenders in children aged 6–10 years

Religion	Caste	Boys		Girls	
		Total aged 6–10 years	Percentage attending school %	Total aged 6–10 years	Percentage attending school %
HINDUS	Kota Brahmins	103	92	97	90
	Other Brahmins	72	97	76	92
	Ganigas and Acharis	57	91	62	69
	Bants	73	76	51	75
	Mogers	165	62	199	34
	Bhillavas	148	59	131	24
	Devadigas	42	67	35	31
	Holeyas	36	28	28	25
	Other Hindus	16	81	10	60
MUSLIMS		26	65	37	31
CHRISTIANS		6	100	12	100
TOTAL		744	71	738	56

boys and girls go to school. Bants come next. About two-thirds of the Moger, Bhillava and Devadiga boys go to school while the proportion of schoolgoers amongst the girls of these castes is much lower. The same is true for the Muslims. Holeyas rank lowest: only about a quarter of their boys and girls go to school.

Family systems and residence patterns

As mentioned above the joint family system has been the traditional living pattern in both the castes which follow the patrilineal and those which adhere to the Aliya Santana mode of inheritance; but this system is now breaking up and many are adopting the nuclear family system. The various religious and caste groups were compared, to examine the relative frequency with which they presented joint and nuclear family living arrangements. Table 3.5 gives the results.

TABLE 3.5

Adoption of joint or nuclear family systems, in religious and caste groups

Religion	*Caste*	*Total number of families*	*Percentage in joint families* %	*Percentage in nuclear families* %
HINDUS	Kota Brahmins	225	40	60
	Other Brahmins	147	35	65
	Ganigas and Acharis	105	42	58
	Bants	113	58	42
	Mogers	297	59	41
	Bhillavas	249	54	46
	Devadigas	66	58	42
	Holeyas	57	44	56
	Other Hindus	23	26	74
MUSLIMS		59	37	63
CHRISTIANS		28	21	79
TOTAL		1369	48	52

Most Christian families are of the nuclear type. Among the patrilineal communities, namely the Brahmins, Acharis, Holeyas, 'other Hindus' and Muslims, nuclear families outnumber the joint families while the opposite is the case for the traditionally matrilineal Bants, Mogers, Devadigas and Bhillavas.

As mentioned earlier, the Aliya Santana system is in a state of transition, and many members of these castes are adopting the patrilocal residence pattern typical of the patrilineal castes. An analysis was carried out to compare, among the various Aliya Santana groups, the proportions of the married couples who continued to live in the traditional pattern: 47 per cent of the married Bants, 52 per cent of the married Devadigas, 37 per cent of the married Holeyas, 68 per cent of the married Bhillavas and 70 per cent of the married Mogers still observed the traditional residence pattern. The greatest change towards patrilocal residence was therefore shown by the Holeyas, while Bhillava and Moger families showed the greatest conservatism in this respect.

4

BRAHMINS, BANTS AND MOGERS

Out of the eleven religious and caste groups in the village, the Kota Brahmins, Bants and Mogers were chosen for a detailed comparison of life styles and any differences in the prevalence of mental disorder (as defined in Chapter 2). The Brahmins were chosen as the ritually highest representative of the patrilineal castes, and the Bants as the ritually highest representative of the Aliya-Santana castes. The Mogers were chosen because though, like the Bants, they follow the Aliya-Santana matrilineal system of inheritance, they are strikingly different from the latter in some other aspects such as their means of livelihood, the strength of their caste bonds, and the relative emancipation of their womenfolk. We set out to determine whether these factors could be related to differences in the prevalence of psychiatric symptoms between the two groups which shared the Aliya-Santana tradition, and between both of these groups and the more prestigious Brahmins.

The socio-demographic survey described in the last chapter had already revealed some of the differences between the three castes. The Mogers are numerically the largest group. The Brahmins are the most educated and the richest. The Bants are more educated than the Mogers but have a comparatively higher proportion living below subsistence level. The Brahmins are mainly landowners, the Bants mainly tenant-cultivators and the Mogers mainly fishermen.

Further study of their life pattern was made through participant observation over a period of one year, at least one member of the team living in the village throughout this period. At the end of the year a questionnaire study was carried out with members of all three castes in order to study their attitudes towards modernisation in general, and in particular to elicit measures of 'social distance' by asking about their readiness to interact socially with members of lower castes.

The origin of the three caste groups

According to legend there were no Brahmins in South Kanara before the 7th century A.D. when the King Mayur-Varma brought them from 'Ahi-Kshetra' (probably the present-day Andhra region) and settled them in 32 villages in this area. There is no historical evidence to support this legend except perhaps a partial and indirect one: local records refer to Brahmins only after the 7th century and not before. The present-day Kota is presumably one of the 32 villages where the immigrant Brahmins were settled.

Bant literally means a soldier or a powerful man. There is evidence that they are the descendants of a group of coastal people who were engaged in prolonged struggles with the large southern kingdoms of the 1st and 2nd centuries A.D. before finally being overpowered by them. In their subsequent history they seem to have withdrawn from armed struggle and built up their influence by concentrating on agriculture. This is still their main occupation though over the years they have lost some of their best lands to the Brahmins. Bants are still a powerful landowning community in most parts of South Kanara, but in Kota and other villages in the Kannada-speaking northern area many of them have been reduced to the status of tenants and agricultural labourers.

Historical records make no special mention of the origin of Mogers; they may well have been living here from prehistoric times.

Religion and its practice

The members of all the three groups call themselves Hindus, believe in caste, Karma and reincarnation, and hold the cow sacred.

Bants and Mogers are demon-worshippers, but the Brahminical tradition forbids animistic practices.

Belief in demons and spirits permeates the life of Bants and Mogers: most of those we talked to could recount the story of a friend or a relative who had suffered the wrath of a demon or was afflicted by a spirit. If there is a bad crop, it must be due to a demon; if there is a bad catch of fish, it might be because a spirit was not properly appeased. Spirits and demons can cause illness, loss of cattle, a quarrel between brothers or a hole in the boat. Even the educated, while bemoaning the irrational beliefs of their less sophisticated brethren, break into a story of the time when they saw something in the dark which could not have been anything but a spirit!

The Brahmins worship all Puranic and Aryan gods and do not align themselves with any exclusive sects such as the Shaivites or Vishnavites. They have a special deity of their own who must be worshipped by an adult male every day, women being excluded from participation in this ritual.

Though the Brahmins deny any belief in demons and spirits, they hold it obligatory to carry out the annual appeasement of the ancestral spirits. Also, it is not uncommon to find the Brahmin taking recourse to the spirit-shrines and consulting the mediums of the village at times of personal distress.

As mentioned earlier, there are a number of temples and Bhuta-sthanas in the village. While the Brahmins, both men and women, go to temples once or twice a week, the Bants and Mogers attend the Bhuta-sthanas. The segregation is, however, far from complete. Bants and Mogers go to the temples very often, and less frequently Brahmin women can be seen at the Bhuta-sthanas.

The young people frequently question the beliefs and rituals of the elders, but in practice we found them to be worshipping the home deity as dutifully and visiting the temples as regularly as their elders.

Food habits

The Brahmins are strict vegetarians, pulses and coconut being their main source of protein. Milk and curds are relished but are available in sufficient quantities only to the rich. Brahmins do not drink alcohol. Most men smoke and a number of women chew tobacco. The food is cooked and served by women, the preparation of food being an elaborate process shared by several persons. The daughters-in-law in the household usually carry out the more exacting tasks of grinding the coconut and cooking the rice. The mother-in-law and the young unmarried girls cook the vegetables. This, however, is not a rigid arrangement and one woman may, when necessary, take up a task usually assigned to another. For example, during the menstrual period, when a woman is considered to be in a polluted state and is not allowed to work inside the house, the other females take up her tasks while she enjoys her monthly holiday.

The Bants and Mogers are meat eaters, but being Hindus, do not eat beef. Meat is, however, expensive and in most houses is seldom eaten more than once a week. Fish is naturally the most common source of protein for the Moger fishermen.

Both Bants and Mogers drink alcohol, the latter much more heavily than the former. Most Mogers drink daily, especially during the fishing season when cash is readily available. Some of them claimed that drinking was 'essential' and helped them withstand the rigours of their occupation.

There is no taboo in either caste against the women's drinking. It is not uncommon to see Moger women drinking at the liquor parlours. The Bant women drink much less and that, too, at home.

Rituals and customs

A Brahmin goes through a series of complicated rituals during his life. There is the birth ceremony, the naming ceremony, the first haircut, the thread ceremony, the marriage, and finally the death ceremony. Even after death he is not left alone, his spirit having to take part in the ancestor worship ceremony conducted by his sons.

Upanayanam, or the thread ceremony, is perhaps the most important ritual for a Brahmin male, signifying as it does his entry into adulthood, and formally ensuring his rights and responsibilities as a Brahmin.

The ritual of Upanayanam starts with a purificatory rite, or 'Prayashchita', during which the boy asks forgiveness for any inadvertent contact with the members of the lower castes during the previous years. This is followed by a haircut and a bath. After this the sacred fire is lit, and halfway through the fire worship the father puts the sacred thread over the boy's shoulder. Once the fire worship has been completed the father whispers the Gayatri-Mantra (a sacred verse) into the boy's ear and the ceremony is over.

At one time this was a four-day affair but now it is completed in a day. Though the times are changing we did not find any Brahmin who had not gone through the ceremony himself or who was not planning to have it performed for his sons.

Bants and Mogers also have ceremonies to mark the occasions of birth,marriage and death, but their rituals are much simpler. There is no upanayanam but instead at the age of 5 both boys and girls go through the ear-piercing ceremony. No special ritual takes place but there is sometimes a small feast. The Mogers also have a 'puberty' ceremony for the girl who is made to sit on five coconuts and is ceremoniously washed by a washerwoman. For her services the latter gets a rupee, a coconut and two pounds of rice. The Bants' ceremonies are performed by a Brahmin priest, but no Brahmin is involved in the Mogers' ceremonies.

Marriage

The usual marriage age for a Brahmin boy is 20–25 years and for a Brahmin girl, 18–22 years. The Bants marry earlier than the Brahmins and the Mogers at an even younger age.

The Brahmins of Kota are divided into four units called 'Gotras', and one can marry only a member of a Gotra other than one's own. Marriage is also permitted with Shivalli Brahmins who are accepted as social equals.

Bants and Mogers are similarly divided into exogamous units called 'Balis'. The rules prohibiting marriage within a Bali are, however, not very rigid among the Mogers.

Cross-cousin marriages are permitted in all the three communities and are fairly common. Tradition says nothing against polygamy but this is rarely practised by any of the groups (the present law of the land forbids it).

Marriages are invariably arranged by the elders. Some of the educated young people dream of 'love-marriage' but it is hardly ever more than a dream. Love affairs do occur, but often have an unhappy ending. Sometimes the elders take the wise step of accepting the youngsters' demands and 'arrange' a marriage with the person of choice if the other conditions—such as his or her membership of a suitable caste and clan, and the compatibility of their horoscopes—are satisfactorily met.

Amongst the Brahmins it is the duty of the parents, and amongst the Bants and Mogers that of the maternal uncle, to search for a good match. Once a possible candidate has been selected, the horoscopes are compared, and no marriage takes place unless the horoscopes are compatible. It is true that the astrologer sometimes obliges by making a suitably generous interpretation of the stars.

Amongst the Brahmins the wedding used to be a 4–5 day affair but is now completed in a day. It has always been much simpler amongst Bants and Mogers. While the wedding is conducted by a Brahmin priest amongst Brahmins and Bants, it is performed by the Gurikara, or Bali-leader, amongst the Mogers.

The girl brings a dowry in all the groups, but the dowry is very modest in the case of the Brahmins, consisting of some jewellery, clothes and household articles. It is even more nominal among the Mogers; but in the Bant caste a very costly dowry is the rule. In fact there is a 'bridegroom price' which is fixed before the wedding. The price depends on the family status, the extent of land-holding and the education of the boy. Cash dowries of up to forty or fifty thousand rupees are often heard of among the few wealthy Bant families, the money going to the family of the boy.

In all three castes, a man is permitted to divorce his wife. A widower may remarry and often does. Widow remarriage and divorce by women are prohibited amongst the Brahmins but permitted amongst the Bants and Mogers. A Brahmin widow is expected to make herself recognisable by shaving her head and wearing a red saree (without the usual upper garment) when she appears in public. She is not supposed to take part in any auspicious ceremony. These restrictions are still observed by the older females but not by the younger ones. No one, however, seems to have had the courage to break the sanction against widow-remarriage.

Strength of caste bonds

A remarkable feature amongst the Mogers is the importance attached to caste ties. Mention has already been made of how the fishermen work in large groups. If someone in a group falls ill or is unable to work for some other genuine reason, he still gets his share of the catch. A form of co-operative insurance also operates, the Bali-leader giving a basic subsistence allowance to the members of his group and offering loans if there is a particularly bad fishing season.

Mogers have their own caste panchayat which decides on disputes between caste members. The first link in the chain of caste judiciary is the Gurikara who looks after the affairs of 20–50 houses allotted to him. The office of the Gurikara is hereditary, and he may try any dispute, civil or criminal, there being agreed punishments for different crimes. If any party does not accept his decision the case is taken to a board consisting of all the Gurikaras of the village. There is a higher court with representatives from four to five villages, and a still higher one for the Taluk. The highest court is the 'Mahajan-Sabha'. This court looks after the interests of all the Mogers of the district and holds its sessions three or four times a year.

The caste court of the Mogers is still a very active system, and it is interesting to see how infrequently the Mogers take their private caste disputes to the public courts. Those we asked gave two reasons for this: fear of the wrath of demons, and fear of being ostracised by others in the group. The latter seemed to be the more important. Mogers work together, share the cost of the boats and accessories, are paid their share even when ill, and are helped by the community leaders when in need. Who would want to lose the benefits of this excellent social security system by breaking the caste rules?

Agriculture, the main occupation of the Brahmins and Bants, does not demand any sharing of work and property—their caste cohesion is therefore not so strong as that of the Mogers. The Brahmins have a bond in their exclusive knowledge of complictaed rituals, and they cherish their traditional status as the highest-ranking caste. There seem to be no comparable pressures for group cohesion amongst the Bants who are known for their rugged independence.

The status of women

Another characteristic which distinguishes the groups is the greater freedom enjoyed by the Moger women as compared with the

Brahmin and Bant women. It is true that all the groups are male-dominated and all the important decisions are made by men. However, amongst the Mogers the women are permitted to go out on their own, to drink in public places and to keep their own money, experiences which are denied to the Brahmin and Bant women. While both Bant and Moger women are permitted to divorce their husbands if there is a sufficient cause, the right is exercised much more often among the Mogers than among the Bants. Though it is equally acceptable in all the three castes for men to beat their wives when displeased with them, it is only the Moger women who are known to hit back with equal ferocity!

All this cannot be explained simply by the facts that Moger women go out to work much more frequently than do women of the other two castes and that they contribute towards the household economy. Many Bant women also go out to work but this does not appear to give them any better status. Nor can the freer role of Moger women be attributed to the Aliya-Santana form of matrilineal inheritance, because this operates among the Bants also. It seemed to us that Bant women cherish their being second only to the Brahmins in ritual status, and hence like to copy some of the latter's social restrictions.

The family

In a traditional joint family it is the oldest male who makes the important decisions. This holds true both in the patrilineal setting of the Brahmins and in the social relationships of the Bants and Mogers, who follow the Aliya-Santana rules of inheritance and residence; in the former the paternal grandfather or senior uncle is the head of the family; in the latter it is the mother's father or her eldest brother. The work on the land is shared, the work in the house is shared, even the clothes are often shared. In infancy, children are looked after by their mothers, but once they are weaned they become part of the group of youngsters looked after by the older girls under the supervision of the oldest female in the household. At about 4 years of age they stop sleeping with their mother and instead sleep with their grandmother. There is often an interesting interplay between the older and the younger generation, with the child being consoled by the grandmother when scolded by the mother, and vice versa.

As mentioned above, both the joint family system and the Aliya-Santana tradition are in the process of being discarded. The shift away from the Aliya-Santana custom is much more evident among the Bants as compared to the Mogers, and that away from the joint family is much commoner among the Brahmins than in either of the other two castes. This is bringing about new relationships, roles, stresses and attitudes, the effects of which are not yet fully apparent.

Caste status

The Brahmins hold the highest ritual rank in the village, while the Bants, though lower than the Brahmins, are considered significantly higher than the Mogers. Traditionally this caste ranking was reinforced by a similar gradation in respect of wealth. This is, however, not so any more. The special help given by the government to the fishing industry has improved the lot of the Mogers, many of whom are now becoming richer than the Bants. It was found that a smaller proportion of Moger than of Bant families was currently living below subsistence level. This has caused considerable insecurity amongst the local Bants and has given rise to some tension between the members of the two castes, which occasionally erupts in scenes of open hostility.

Social distance and modernisation

During the first three months of March 1971 a questionnaire study was carried out to compare the three castes with respect to their willingness to mix with the members of other, lower castes, and their readiness to express opinions critical of the traditional customs and beliefs. We also wanted to see whether the younger people held more liberal and modern views than the older, and whether the old-young difference of attitudes was greater in any one of the three castes.

Social distance scale

Following the classical technique of Bogardus (1959), which was elaborated in the Indian context by Pauline Mahar (1959), a social distance scale was constructed using three questions designed to elicit a greater or lesser degree of willingness to mix with the lower castes. The three questions inquired about the respondents' willingness to enter the house of a member of a named lower-caste group, to eat in such a house, or to arrange a marriage with one of that community. These questions were asked in relation to members of five castes—Bhillavas, Devadigas, Acharis, Ganigas and Holeyas —all ritually lower than the Brahmins, Bants and Mogers. The replies yielded a score on this social distance scale.

Modernity questionnaire

Smith and Inkeles (1966) have described a set of personal qualities which are typical of a 'modern' as contrasted with a tradition-oriented man. These qualities are (a) an openness to new experience, (b) assertion of independence from the authority of traditional figures, (c) belief in the efficacy of science and medicine, (d) high occupational and educational ambitions for oneself and one's children, (e) concern for planned action, (f) interest in civic and community affairs and (g) an interest in national and international affairs. This profile of a 'modern' man has been shown to be valid for different cultures and nationalities.

We agree in principle with this concept of a 'modern' man but feel that in any empirical investigation the items reflecting these qualities should be pertinent to the local context. With this in mind we chose a set of seventeen topics of special relevance to the people of Kota and with respect to which 'traditional' and a 'modern' view could be clearly defined. A questionnaire incorporating these topics was prepared, in which the questions were framed in such a manner that a positive answer would sometimes reflect a traditional view and sometimes a modern view in a purely random fashion. This guarded against the well-known bias towards answering any questions in the affirmative. The items were as follows:

1. Widow remarriage. 2. Divorce by men. 3. Divorce by women. 4. Love marriage. 5. Age at which girls should get married. 6. Dowry. 7. Unitary vs. Joint family. 8. Aliya-Santana System. 9. Higher education for women. 10. Outside paid employment for women. 11. Permission for women to go out of the house alone. 12. Wife eating food before the husband. 13. Use of modern agricultural methods. 14. Family planning. 15. Emigration in search of work. 16. Belief in devils and spirits. 17. Belief in the efficacy of prayer.

The social distance scale and the modernisation questionnaire were given to 120 randomly selected adult members of the three castes. Six out of the 360 potential respondents (two Brahmins and four Bants—all females) did not co-operate in the inquiry, giving a response rate of 98 per cent.

Results

Social distance

The social distance measure fulfilled the requirements of a Guttman scale, that is to say, it was both unidimensional and cumulative. A score of '1' was given for every 'yes' answer and one of '0' for every 'no' answer. The scores for the three questions were then added up to give the total distance score for each respondent. A higher score indicates a greater willingness to mix with lower castes.

Analysis was carried out to test the effect of sex, caste, age and education on the social distance score. The results of the analysis are given in Table 4.1 and can be summarised as follows:

TABLE 4.1

Factors related to social distance scores

	No.	Mean score	S.D.		Significance
1. *Sex and social distance*				't'	
Males	139	1·82	·776	2·54	p < ·05
Females	215	1·63	·558		
2. *Caste and social distance*				'F'	
Males					
Brahmins	39	1·21	·951	22·03	p < ·001
Bants	44	2·11	·493		
Mogers	56	2·00	·572		
Females					
Brahmins	79	1·13	·589	54·33	p < ·001
Bants	72	1·87	·662		
Mogers	64	1·88	·390		
3. *Age and social distance*				't'	
Brahmin males					
Young (30 or less)	17	1·55	·858	2·75	p < ·01
Old (31 or more)	22	0·76	·903		
Brahmin females					
Young (30 or less)	43	1·28	·701	2·49	p < ·05
Old (31 or more)	36	0·88	·516		

No statistically significant difference was observed between the young and the old of the other two castes.

	No.	Mean score	S.D.		Significance
4. *Education and social distance*				't'	
Males					
Low education	56	2·02	·665	2·34	p < ·05
High education	83	1·71	·810		
Females					
Low education	154	1·68	·557	2·15	p < ·05
High education	61	1·49	·649		

1. Sex: Males had a higher mean score compared with the females.

2. Caste: The mean social distance scores of the three caste groups were compared. It was found that the Brahmins, both males and females, scored low, while Bants and Mogers had very similar, high scores.

3. Age: Those below 30 were compared with those above 30 for

each caste and sex group. It was found that the young Brahmins, both males and females, scored higher than their elders. No difference was observed between the scores of young and old members of the other two castes.

4. Education: Those having primary schooling or less were compared with those who had had better education. Education did not seem to influence the scores of Bants and Mogers, but the better educated Brahmins (both males and females) had higher scores than those who were less educated.

Modernity score

It was decided to derive a summated 'modernity score' from the questionnaire mentioned above. As a first step, the items on which there was more than 80 per cent agreement, whether 'in-favour' or 'against' were omitted since they did not help to discriminate between those with a bias towards modernity or traditionalism.

An attempt was then made to make the scale unidimensional, and therefore those items which did not have a statistically significant positive correlation with the total score were also omitted. These two pruning operations left eleven out of the original seventeen items. (The items omitted were Nos. 2, 6, 8, 11, 13 and 15 above.) A 'modern' response to each of the eleven questions was given a score of '1' and a traditional response a score of '0'. The scores for the eleven items were then added up to give a total modernity score for each respondent. A higher score indicates a greater readiness to hold 'modern' views.

As for the social distance scale, an analysis was carried out to test the effect of sex, caste, age and education on the modernity score. The results are given in Table 4.2 and can be summarised as follows:

1. Sex: The males have a higher score than the females.

2. Caste: Among males, the Brahmins have the highest, Bants the next highest and Mogers the lowest scores. Among females, Brahmins again have the highest score but there is very little difference between Bants and Mogers.

3. Age: Except for the Brahmin females, where the younger have a significantly higher score than the older, age shows no relation with the modernity score.

4. Education: Those with better education, both males and females, have a higher score than those with less education. The difference persists when the comparison is carried out separately for the different caste and sex groups.

To examine the relative significance of education and caste, caste

TABLE 4.2

Factors related to modernity scores

	No.	Mean score	S.D.		Significance
1. *Sex and modernity*				't'	
Males	139	5·51	2·41	8·23	p < ·001
Females	215	3·51	2·11		
2. *Caste and modernity*				'F'	
Males					
Brahmins	39	6·79	2·48	11·62	p < ·001
Bants	44	5·59	2·35		
Mogers	56	4·54	1·98		
Females					
Brahmins	79	4·32	2·82	8·06	p < ·001
Bants	42	3·17	1·68		
Mogers	64	1·42	1·41		
3. *Age and modernity*				't'	
Brahmin females					
Young (30 or less)	43	5·04	2·92	2·90	p < ·01
Old (31 or more)	36	3·11	2·19		
No statistically significant difference was found in the young and old Brahmin males or the young and old of the other two castes.					
4. *Education and modernity*				't'	
Males					
High education	56	6·65	3·93	4·7	p < ·001
Low education	83	4·21	1·82		
Females					
High education	159	4·63	2·75	5·17	p < ·001
Low education	61	3·06	1·59		

comparisons were carried out separately for the high and low education groups. It was found that the caste differences in the mean scores were much reduced in the 'high education' males, and disappeared completely among those of low education. This shows that the high scores of the Brahmins are attributable more to their higher level of education than to any other factor.

To summarise, the Brahmins, though more modern than the Bants and Mogers in several respects, show the least willingness to mix with the lower castes. The younger and more educated Brahmins expressed a greater willingness in this regard than the older and less educated Brahmins; but their 'social distance' scores were still less than those of the Mogers and the Bants. Age and education do very little to alter the attitudes of the Mogers and Bants.

Education is the single most important determinant of modernity. The high modernity scores of the Brahmins seem to be due to their being more educated than members of the other two castes.

5

PROFESSIONAL HEALERS IN KOTA

Traditional and modern healers

To whom does one turn when in pain, sickness and distress? Traditionally the people of Kota, not discriminating between physical illness, mental illness and suffering of other kinds, have taken their troubles to the temple priests or to itinerant holy men, but most of all to three kinds of professional healers: Vaids, Mantarwadis and Patris. We refer to them as professionals because, unlike the priests and holy men who exercise their healing power through God's grace and dispense it free of charge, the Vaids, Mantarwadis and Patris all claim to have undergone a period of training to achieve their expertise and charge a fee for their services.

There are 23 such traditional healers in the village but now their ranks have been joined by doctors trained in Western medicine. The first doctor came to the village in the early 1930s and died in 1966. The second came in the 1950s and is still practising though not very actively. The third came in 1965 and over the subsequent eight years has built up a lucrative practice which covers many villages besides Kota. Besides these 'private' doctors who charge for their services, a free medical service is provided at the government Primary Health Centre. This centre though situated in Kota is intended to serve a population of 68,000 spread over 31 villages. It has a doctor, two health visitors, two family planning instructors, eight midwives, and seven basic health workers. The main tasks of the basic health workers are to visit each family at least once a month, giving simple instruction in the principles of preventive medicine, and to take part in anti-malarial and anti-tuberculosis programmes. They are as yet too few to carry out once-a-month family visits throughout their area, but there is provision for more posts which are expected to be filled in due course.

The centre has a mobile dispensary and recently a 25-bed in-patient unit has also been added.

The conceptual framework of the traditional healers' practice

The Vaids are practitioners of Ayurveda, an indigenous system of empirical medicine with a vast pharmacopoeia. This system is believed to have originated in India more than 3000 years ago and is described in one of the four Vedas—a set of holy scriptures which the Hindus believe to have been received directly from the gods. Whatever its origin, it is a logical system—that is, once one accepts its premises. Very briefly, an illness, according to Vaidic concepts, is due to an imbalance between the natural elements, the imbalance leading to an excess of heat, cold, bile, wind or fluid secretions in the body. These bodily disturbances then singly or in combination give rise to symptoms, which can be physical or mental. In the psychic sphere, excessive heat for example can cause excitement, excessive cold can cause depression, and excessive bile can cause hostility. The imbalance of natural elements which starts this whole chain reaction may itself be caused by a variety of environmental factors, such as eating 'wrong' food, or uninhibited sexual indulgence. There is also a place in this system for *pishachis*, or evil spirits, which may cause mental illness or fits by possessing an individual. Treatment is effected through herbs, roots and pills—all designed to redress the bodily imbalance.

This system declined during the centuries of Mogul and British dominance but has been revived once again by the Indian national government. There is much talk of getting rid of its irrational elements and developing what is best in it. Many Institutes now offer a diploma or a degree in Ayurveda. Extensive research is being conducted to test scientifically the many herbal and medicinal potions described in the Vaidic texts. It may be mentioned that 'Rauwolfia Serpentina', the plant whose extract is now widely used in Western medicine for the treatment of hypertension (and was extensively used as a major tranquilliser before being replaced by modern psychotropic drugs) was employed in Vaidic medicine for centuries before being introduced to the West.

The term 'healer' does not sufficiently describe the role of the *Mantarwadis* and the *Patris*, whose work extends far beyond the treatment of the sick, to include such things as improving business prospects, finding lost cattle, propitiating the rain gods at times of drought or flood, increasing the yield of a cow, or pacifying a child who cries too much. In fact they deal with any cause of distress for which the villager can recognise no practical remedy, or which he believes to be due to powers beyond his control.

Both Mantarwadis and Patris work on the principle that all troubles (such as natural disasters, financial losses, interpersonal quarrels, diseases) are the result of past misdeeds, individual or collective, committed by the suffering person or persons themselves or their near kin, either in their present life or in a previous existence. There is no escape from the consequences of a misdeed, which is always punished. Every villager knows that sooner or later Shiva, the god of destruction, will exact retribution, either through the agency of one of the spirits and Bhutas at his command or by bringing about a malign conjunction of the stars.

What counts as a misdeed is usually a breach of the community's customs or taboos. Though generally the lesser spirits and Bhutas act under the command of higher beings, sometimes they are prompted by a personal grievance: for example, one might have forgotten to appease a particular spirit or one might have inadvertently humiliated a Bhuta by knocking down an anthill in which he was residing. It is, therefore, possible to commit a misdeed unwittingly, and even the best of citizens, who have always obeyed the community codes with respect, could incite the wrath of a spirit or Bhuta by mistake. The most exemplary ethical conduct does not ensure that one will not be punished for a misdeed committed in a previous life. Further, a Bhuta might exact vengeance for something done by one's dead ancestors or by one's relatives in their present or previous lives. It is also believed that some evil people learn the secret of commanding a spirit or Bhuta, and can direct them to wreak mischief on others. (These evil people would, of course, themselves be punished eventually, either in their present existence, or in future lives.)

This all-embracing conceptual system ensures that absolutely no-one can consider himself immune from suffering.

The actual nature of the suffering depends on the particular conjunction of the stars (some conjunctions causing illness, others floods or droughts) or on the personality of the acting Bhuta or spirit. Some Bhutas are just playful and are content with bringing down the houseroof; others are more malign and revel in inflicting disease and death. Occasionally the spirit or the Bhuta may decide to take residence in the body of its victim who as a result becomes 'possessed' and starts to behave in a manner characteristic of the invading demon. The spirit may take up permanent residence and cause madness, or it may go in and out of the body causing 'fits' at each entry and departure.

The account given above is culled from interviews with several Mantarwadis and Patris who did not necessarily agree on details. Also, quite often when shown logical faults in their argument they would offer explanations which apparently were inspired on the spur of the moment. They were all, however, staunchly agreed on the fundamental issue, that most suffering is a punishment for past misdeeds, a belief shared by the majority of the population not only in Kota but all over India.

Though the Mantarwadis and Patris are agreed about how suffering is caused, they differ in their procedures for divining the 'cause' in a particular case and in their methods of resolving the problem.

A Mantarwadi is a master of the zodiac and of the potent secret mystical verses termed mantras. It is through the zodiac that he discovers the cause of the problem and it is through the mantras that he relieves it. There are different mantras for different spirits and demons, some more potent than others. It is the potency of the mantra which decides the fee—there being mantras for keeping the trouble away for a week, a month, a year or for ever. Rarely does the Mantarwadi effect a permanent removal of the trouble— this is a costly operation and as one of them admitted with a wry smile: '. . . the days are bad and I would not want to lose my client by making him completely better'. In actual practice a Mantarwadi, after looking at the zodiac, explains to the client the faulty actions which have 'caused' his trouble and suggests a penance for his misdeeds. To strengthen the benefits of the penance he also gives a thread, or a talisman powered by the mantra, and sometimes the ash from a leaf on which the sacred mantra was etched before it was burned.

The work pattern of a Mantarwardi might become clearer if we give an account of a session we spent with an expert who lived a few miles from Kota and was well renowned all over South Kanara.

We were told that it was not necessary to fix an appointment with this famous man. However, when we went to see him one Monday he was busy in his vegetable garden. He explained that his 'powers' left him on a Monday and invited us to come along the following Sunday.

On Sunday we found him ready at 9 a.m. waiting for us before starting his clinic. There was nothing special about the decor of the clinic which was an ordinary room with a desk, a chair and a rather prominent clock. There were about 20 clients who, it seemed, had been waiting patiently since the early hours of the morning. Without even looking at them the Mantarwadi sat down on the only chair in the room (a bench was soon brought in for us) and started drawing with a chalk the zodiac chart for the day on the desk in front of him.

Having completed this chart he casually summoned the client sitting nearest and from the clock checked the exact time the client came face to face with him. With a wave of the hand he forbade the man from talking—as he evidently wanted to do—about his present misery. The next few minutes were spent in some further calculations while the client waited patiently. Having finished the calculations the Mantarwadi spoke out with a clear commanding voice: 'You are 60, you come from a place where the fish abound and you want relief from the pains and aches which have been haunting you for a long time.' 'And fever,' said the client. 'And fever,' agreed the Mantarwadi. A total silence prevailed among the other clients during this discourse, which ended with the client's face lighting up with reverence and his begging to be told the cause of his trouble. A few more minutes were spent on calculation, after which the Mantarwadi spoke out once again with the same commanding voice: 'Is it true or is it not that your father is dead?' 'Yes,' agreed the client. 'Then is it true or is it not that during the last three years at least once you did not complete the ritual of Shraddha?'* The client hung his head down and acquiesced meekly. 'Well this is what comes of not attending to your dead ancestors. You will need to arrange a ritual feast to which at least five Brahmins must be invited. You will have to go to Dharmasthala and bathe in the holy water. And here is a thread which you must wear on your aching knees.' Saying this he held out a piece of string, whispered a mantra over it and gave it to the man.

The man folded his hands, touched his forehead to the ground in front of the healer, and left after putting a rupee note on the desk.

The next client was a young man of 20 whom the healer diagnosed as being in love with the neighbour's daughter and as suffering from sexual weakness. The treatment was a mantra-powered talisman which would only remove the sexual weakness. The question of the young woman was left for the next interview, a fortnight later, when the stars were expected to be more favourable.

During the morning session (lasting about 4 hours) the Mantarwadi saw 32 cases. Only one-third had come for their own problems —others came to give the complaints of relatives and friends who could not come themselves for various reasons.

The complaints could be categorised as follows:

1.	Business losses	6
2.	Fits	4
3.	Sexual weakness	4
4.	Physical weakness	4
5.	Madness	3
6.	Cough and fever	3

* Appeasement of ancestral spirits.

7. Persistently poor catch of fish   3
8. Skin disease   2
9. Persistent failure in school   1
10. Constant strife in the family   2

Total   32

The 'causes' of the complaints could be categorised as follows:

1. 'Jakani' (spirit of a dead child)   8
2. Bhutas (all named)   4
3. Unfavourable stars   5
4. Displeased ancestral spirits   12
5. Physical illness   3

To those the Mantarwadi diagnosed as suffering from physical illness, he expressed his inability to help and advised them to go to a nearby hospital. One of them was an obvious case of epilepsy and the other two suffered from cough and fever (probably tuberculosis). None of the 'mad' cases were referred to the hospital.

As treatment, some sort of penance was prescribed for six people, a visit to Dharmasthala temple for four people, and some sort of thread, ash or talisman was given to all.

The fees ranged from 20 paisa to Rs 10—all displayed on the desk. The fees were offered by the clients depending on their own economic status, and in no case did the healer make any special demands. Except for one case no-one was specifically asked to come again.

Some of the observations which appeared to us as particularly striking are given below:

1. The personality of the Mantarwadi: a high-browed, tall, muscular man with a glowing skin, shiny eyes and clear loud voice.

2. Lack of privacy: everyone's complaints and treatment were discussed openly, before the audience of waiting clients, and no-one made any attempt to conceal the actual amount of the fees paid.

3. Respect for the healer: the healer was as often wrong as right in his announcement of the complaint but the clients did not seem to mind, and prompted him with their real complaints if he went wrong.

4. The effect of the explanation: the people seemed to be more interested in the cause of their trouble rather than its nature. As soon as the cause was explained to them they seemed as if vindicated.

5. The acceptance of the 'medical' model: it was indeed interesting to note that both the healer as well as his clients accepted the possibility of a physical cause as casually as a 'spiritual' cause, and that the healer seemed to accept the hospital as supplementary to rather than competitive with his trade.

A Patri does not claim any special knowledge or powers except his ability to act as a medium for a spirit or a Bhuta who is supposed to conduct the actual therapeutic session. The only expertise a Patri claims is in knowing the ritual for inviting and being possessed by the Bhuta or the spirit whose servant he is.

A Patri has no knowledge of astrology. The first 'screening' for the cause is conducted with the help of a handful of shells or rice grains which the Patri picks out from a heap in front of him. A spirit or a Bhuta is declared to be the source of the trouble if the shells or the rice grains picked out add up to an even number. If a spirit or Bhuta is the cause (which is invariably stated) the Patri closes his eyes, praying to his own tutelary spirit or Bhuta, asking him to infuse therapeutic power into the thread or talisman which he is holding in his hand. This activated thread or talisman is then given to the client.

If the problem is more serious the treatment is carried out through a Darshana ceremony. To the beat of drums, accompanying the ritual worship of the Bhuta, and amidst the fragrance of incense and areca palm flowers, the Patri goes into a trance and becomes possessed by his master Bhuta. All further work is now carried out by the master Bhuta who uses the Patri's body and voice only as a means of communication. The spirit which is troubling the client is now beckoned by the master Bhuta, asked to manifest itself and not hide shamefully behind the body of a mere human being. After some further music, the client starts to tremble and soon breaks into a weird dance. Suddenly the dance stops, the spirit or the Bhuta which is the cause of the mischief announces itself with a shrill noise—much like an epileptic cry. A dialogue then follows between the master Bhuta (of the Patri) and the offending spirit (of the client). If the master Bhuta is more powerful than the culprit spirit he orders the latter to leave the body of the client. However, if the latter is more powerful (local folklore gives detailed accounts of the respective powers of the various demons and spirits) the master Bhuta pleads, asking the other to state its conditions for releasing the client. The client's Bhuta declares its conditions (an animal sacrifice, a ritual feast or a 'house' for its use) and after this both the Patri and the client, throwing a final fit, foaming at the mouth, pass into unconsciousness. Neither of them remembers anything of what transpired during the Darshana, but the onlookers do and prepare to carry out the necessary conditions. The Patri gets a small fee for his services.

Sometimes the client gets 'cured', sometimes he does not. In the latter case further Darshanas are performed, more conditions are fulfilled and, if the mischievous Bhuta still continues to give trouble, the client is taken to the Dharmasthala temple where the master of the master demons—the greatest of all, in front of whom all the spirits and Bhutas shudder—relieves the client of his misery once and for all. This ceremony is understandably very expensive.

The traditional healers of Kota

Out of the 23 traditional healers in Kota, two are Vaids, three are Mantarwadis, four are Patris, and the other fourteen claim to know both about Mantras and Darshanas and call themselves 'Patri-Mantrik'.

The Vaids and the three 'pure' Mantarwadis are all Brahmins. The Patris and the Patri-Mantriks belong to the lower castes except one who is a Brahmin. For all of them the profession of healing is a part-time occupation. They all agreed that since the arrival of doctors they could not support themselves and their families on the earnings of their practice alone. Some have their own land, some are priests in the temple, but a number of the Patris and Patri-Mantriks are also agricultural labourers.

For 19 out of the 23, healing was a hereditary profession; the other four started training in it either after they were 'possessed' at an early age or had been 'told' in a dream that they should practice healing.

The Vaids and the 'pure' Mantarwadis are more popular than the Patris and the Patri-Mantriks. All of them without exception acknowledge the achievements of science and modern medicine, but claim that their treatment can 'strengthen' the effects of the drugs given by the doctors. None of them, however, wanted his sons to follow in his footsteps. 'Times are changing', they said.

The modern doctors

As mentioned before, there are two private practitioners and one salaried doctor in the village. The salaried doctor is obliged not to charge for his services; however, it is not he but one of the private practitioners who is most popular amongst the Kota people. This is a hard-working, pleasant man who entertained us several times during our stay in the village.

He works from 8 a.m. until late at night and makes domiciliary visits. There is a fixed charge for the domiciliary visit, but in the dispensary money is charged for the medicine given and not for consultation. He treats all kinds of cases, but admits to knowing very little about psychiatric problems. This is not surprising since hardly any psychiatry is taught in the undergraduate curricula of most Indian medical colleges. He categorised the mentally ill broadly into two groups, hysterics and depressives. On further inquiry it was found that he limited the diagnosis of hysteria to those having convulsive fits, and his description of the depressives turned out to be that of a typical schizophrenic. He had used minor tranquillisers and major tranquillisers as well as anti-depressants in his practice. According to his account he always tried minor tranquillisers first, then major tranquillisers and, if neither of these worked, he tried anti-depressants. He persistently stressed the limitations of his knowledge and his wish to learn more, if only he had more time. His predicament seemed understandable; he really had very little opportunity to learn more. The nearest mental hospital is 250 miles away, and the nearest trained psychiatrist (the only one in the entire South Kanara district) is 70 miles away in Mangalore. Not many patients are willing to travel so far and pay the high fees of a specialist. In the meantime he struggles on, sharing his psychiatric patients with the traditional healers and managing to preserve a bland expression when his patients claim to being treated simultaneously by a Mantarwadi. The present trend is for most physically ill patients to consult a modern doctor first and soon follow it up with consultation with 'a traditional healer if the doctor's medicine does not take effect immediately. The contradictory 'causal' terminology used by the doctors and the traditional healers apparently presents no problem to a Kota villager. 'There are many ways to truth' claimed a university educated Brahmin, echoing the core philosophy of Hinduism, which effortlessly embraces contradictions.

Times, however, are changing. The rationalism taught at schools, the propaganda of the health workers, but most of all the beneficial effects of modern medicines make people question the efficacy of traditional healers more and more; though most of them still believe that Bhutas and spirits exist and bring misfortunes (38 per cent of the men and 80 per cent of the women believed this to be true, in the study of attitudes towards modernisation mentioned in the previous chapter) not many agree that the traditional healers are the best agencies of help in case of illness.

Traditional or modern? A study of attitudes

To obtain a clearer picture of public attitudes towards using the different kinds of healers available in the village, a questionnaire study was carried out at the same time as the studies on social distance and modernisation, and with the same sample of respondents. A check list of common symptoms and problems encountered in the 'clinics' of the traditional healers was provided, and people were asked to which of the given healers they would go first if they themselves or their family members complained of any of the items in the check list. The respondents were allowed to indicate a Mantarwadi, a Patri, a Vaid, a doctor or a temple priest as their first choice, but were also permitted to say that they would not seek help from any of these healers.

Except for loss of cattle, and business losses (where most of the respondents did not want to take any action at all) and for possession (where the Mantarwadis and Patris were highly favoured), the modern doctors emerged as the clear winners with respect to every complaint. More than three-quarters of this sample of the population would consult a doctor first if they or their near ones suffered from fits, bodily weakness, sexual weakness or sleeplessness; more than half would go to a doctor first for advice about states of excitement or withdrawal. In contrast, more than half (both men and women) would consult a Patri or a Mantarwadi if they or their near ones became 'possessed'. It is interesting to note that in general women are more in favour of taking some action as compared to men and also show a higher preference for modern doctors. This latter result is somewhat surprising since one would expect the higher 'modernity' score of the men to be accompanied by a greater preference for the modern doctors. That these expressed attitudes do reflect the 'real' attitudes was, however, borne out by the fact that in the main population survey women were found to consult the modern doctors more often than men.

Further analysis was carried out to examine caste differences and the effect of age and education on attitudes towards utilisation of modern doctors. However, since we were mainly interested in the symptoms of mental disorder, this further analysis was limited to attitudes in respect of fits, states of excitement or withdrawal or possession, sexual weakness and sleeplessness.

No statistically significant caste differences were observed in cases of fits; both men and women in all three castes agreed that this was a matter for the doctor. With regard to the other symptoms, however, there were differences of opinion. Table 5.1 shows the

TABLE 5.1

Preference for doctor as first source of help for various symptoms: caste and sex differences

Symptom category	Brahmins	Bants	Mogers
	%	%	%
Excitement			
Males	59	64	32
Females	70	81	67
Withdrawal			
Males	51	52	34
Females	15	58	52
Sexual weakness			
Males ·	77	84	55
Females	63	83	72
Sleeplessness			
Males	69	86	66
Females	77	91	75
Possession			
Males	18	—	—
Females	—	—	—

proportion preferring doctors as the first person they would go to if they or a member of their family suffered from excitement, withdrawal, sexual weakness, sleeplessness or possession.

18 per cent of Brahmin men thought that a 'possessed' person should first be taken to a doctor, but none of the other respondents shared this view. For all other symptoms, Mogers (both men and women) showed the lowest tendency to consult a doctor while the Bants showed the highest.

Except for sleeplessness, for which those above 30 showed a greater preference for consulting a modern doctor than did the younger people (perhaps because of a greater experience of the problem of sleeplessness), the attitudes of older and younger respondents did not show any statistically significant difference in their preference for modern doctors. This was true for both males and females.

For all symptoms both men and women who had more than primary education showed a statistically significant higher preference for modern doctors, as compared with the less educated.

It is evident that the traditional forms of succour offered by Vaids, Mantarwadis and Patris are still resorted to by many villagers, and that a majority of both men and women of Kota would turn first to a Mantarwadi or a Patri should a case of 'possession' occur in their family. Nevertheless, awareness is spreading about the efficacy of

Western medicine. More highly educated villagers showed a greater readiness to consult modern doctors than did the less educated; but surprisingly the women, in spite of being less educated than the men, and in most respects more conservative, actually consulted doctors more often than did their menfolk.

6

DEVELOPING THE PSYCHIATRIC INTERVIEW SCHEDULES

While attempts were being made in Kota to investigate the socio-anthropological characteristics of its people, work was in progress at the All India Institute of Mental Health and its associated mental hospital to design and standardise a structured interview schedule, which would finally be used in the Kota population survey. The whole exercise, which took nearly two years, passed through the following stages:

1. The development of the Indian Psychiatric Interview Schedule (IPIS).

2. A pilot field survey in a small village near Bangalore. The survey was to examine the feasibility of a two-stage procedure: an initial screening followed by a detailed examination of likely positive cases with the IPIS. This pilot study prompted the next stage:

3. The development of the Indian Psychiatric Survey Schedule (IPSS) which could be used directly without an initial screening.

A detailed exposition of the various pilot studies and the reliability studies which were carried out in the two-year period is given elsewhere (Kapur *et al.*, 1974). This chapter gives a condensed account.

The development of the Indian Psychiatric Interview Schedule (IPIS)

Our aim was to develop an instrument which would put special emphasis on symptoms common in the Indian context. With this in view our first step was to examine the case records of 285 Kannada-speaking patients aged 15 or more who had attended the out-patient department of the Bangalore mental hospital during the months of May and June 1970. A retrospective study of this kind was not expected to give a complete and accurate account of the array of symptoms experienced by such patients, but the information collected from these case records was sufficient to prepare a provisional interview schedule which was then prospectively tried out with a group of 40 new outpatients.

Each of these 40 patients was first interviewed using the provisional schedule, and then a routine unstructured clinical interview was carried out. The information obtained through the structured and unstructured interviews was compared, and the provisional schedule was revised to include new items and to frame the questions in such a manner as to be easily understood by the illiterate villagers who formed the bulk of the hospital's clientele.

The revised schedule was tried out with another group of 40 new patients, but this time, in addition to the interview with the patient, an inquiry was also conducted with a close relative or a friend of each patient. An analysis was carried out to compare the symptoms reported by the patients and those described by their informants. The results of this analysis are shown in Table 6.1.

TABLE 6.1

A comparison of the symptoms from 40 patients and their informants

Symptoms from the patients	Frequency (%)	Symptoms from the informants	Frequency (%)
Sleeplessness	20	Sleeplessness	50
Giddiness	15	Ununderstandable speech	35
Headache	15		
Fear	15	Poor appetite	28
Pain in legs	13	Violent	23
Burning sensations	13	Does not work	23
Indigestion	13		
		Wanders away	18
Exhaustion	10	Laughs to himself	18
Heaviness in head	10	Abusive	18
Forgetfulness	10		
Muscular tension	10	Bizarre behaviour	10
		Withdrawn	10
Poor appetite	8	Poor memory, destructive	8
		suspicions, self neglect	8
Backache, palpitation, sweating, loss of interest, numbness, itching, poverty of thought, worries, night emissions, tremors, depression, dullness, suicidal idea, irritability	5 or less each	Disorientation Homicidal Excessive drinking Hallucinations Delusions	5 or less each

It is interesting to see that while the patients report symptoms of subjective distress, the informants report symptoms of nuisance value to others. This should surprise no one, but what is indeed surprising is the fact that almost all well-known research instruments concentrate on an interview with the patient only, thus missing out important information which can be obtained from a relative or a friend who has been in close contact with the patient.

A new provisional schedule was constructed and this had three sections: (1) structured interview with an informant; (2) structured interview with the patient; and (3) standardised observation by the investigator.

A study was carried out to examine the inter-investigator reliability of the schedule. A member of the research team, Mrs Malavika Kapur (clinical psychologist) and the deputy medical superintendent of the mental hospital, Dr S. M. Channabasavanna (psychiatrist) took part in this reliability study. 40 patients were seen in all: 20 of these patients were interviewed by each investigator, and while one conducted the interview, *both* recorded the presence or absence of symptoms independently.

Agreement was found to be very high between the investigators on sections I and II, but for the third section, which consisted of clinical observations by the investigators, agreement was low. Out of the total 1360 ratings in this section the investigators disagreed on 205.

The items for which positive agreement (both investigators claiming the symptom to be present) was lower than disagreement were dropped, and a new version of the schedule was prepared. Another reliability study was carried out with a new set of 40 patients, and this time the frequency of inter-rater disagreement was found to be statistically insignificant.

Subsequent to this second reliability study another section of historical information was added to the schedule, consisting of ten questions with precoded answers. This final version of the schedule was named the Indian Psychiatric Interview Schedule (IPIS).

The IPIS includes questions to ascertain the presence or absence of 124 psychiatric symptoms; its administration requires 45–90 minutes and it can be used only by trained psychiatrists. As such it is impractical for use in a large scale population survey.

Field investigators are familiar with the dilemma that techniques which ensure a comprehensive inquiry are too costly, in terms of time, effort and expertise required to be usable. A commonly accepted compromise is to conduct a rapid initial screening of the total population and then follow it up with a detailed investigation of the 'suspects'. We wondered whether a similar strategy could be adopted in the Kota survey. With this in view a screening questionnaire was prepared with two sections: the first with 22 questions on the respondent's own mental state, and the other with 21 questions relating to any one in the family or village who in the respondent's opinion might be suffering from one or more of the given check-list of symptoms. It was decided to use this questionnaire in a pilot field survey and then give the IPIS to anyone with a positive score on one or more of the items. The survey was carried out in a village named Sakalwada with a population of just under 500 persons.

The Sakalwada pilot field survey

Sakalwada is a small village about 22 km from Bangalore. It was selected because of its nearness to Bangalore and because it was of a convenient size for a pilot project.

The initial contact

During the month of July 1971 several visits were made to the village and an attempt was made to contact the doctor at the local health centre, the basic health worker and some important members of the village community. These community leaders were informed about the purpose of the survey, and they all promised to co-operate as well as to encourage the others in the village to take part in the inquiry. It was announced that anyone found to be in need of more advanced medical treatment would be referred to a specialist in the Bangalore Hospital.

The survey

The screening questionnaire was given by Mr Eshwar to the men and by Mrs Kapur to the women. The IPIS was given by Dr Sayeed Ahmed to men and by Mrs Kapur once again to the women. Dr Kapur supervised the inquiry and was consulted whenever problems arose. The women and old retired men were generally seen during the day and the working men in the evening. The inquiry was limited to adults aged 15 or more.

During the first few days the respondents were brought for interview to a makeshift office in the local school, but this proved to be cumbersome and a house-to-house investigation was started. At first we were concerned about the lack of privacy in the Indian village houses, but this did not turn out to be as bad as we had feared. Often a private corner could be found; sometimes the respondent helped by clearing off the others and occasionally we ourselves took courage and asked the onlookers to leave, promising a similar privacy when their turn came.

As we reached half way through the survey it was discovered that:

(a) the screening questionnaire had a very low threshold, so that the IPIS had to be given to 80 per cent of the respondents. The essential purpose of the screening (i.e. to reduce substantially the number of those requiring detailed interview) was therefore not being served.

(b) It was often very difficult to persuade people to undergo a second interview.

(c) in the field situation, the IPIS took on an average only 15–20 minutes to complete. This was because the average respondent in the village had many fewer symptoms than the average patient in the hospital setting.

Because of these findings we decided to conduct the rest of the inquiry directly with the more detailed instrument. It had to be modified, however; certain items were dropped, the order of questions was changed, the criteria for an interview with the informant were revised, and the section on inquiry about others (originally a part of the screening questionnaire) was added on to the main schedule. These modifications were brought about almost from day to day as we had more and more experience of interviewing the villagers.

The new version of the schedule was designated the Indian Psychiatric Survey Schedule (IPSS) and is described in the next section of this chapter.

Results

Out of the 239 adults (those aged 15 or above) in the village only 5 (all women) refused to co-operate. 35 per cent of the men and 31 per cent of the women had one or more psychiatric symptoms. This showed a level of symptom prevalence as high as in most studies conducted in the West. The individual frequencies of the various symptoms are given in Table 6.2.

It can be seen that 'vague somatic symptoms' (without demonstrable organic pathology) and symptoms of sleep and appetite disturbance were among the highest reported. Irritability, exhaustion and subjective forgetfulness were high amongst men, while women complained of headache more often than men.

The frequency of the depressive group of symptoms was also very high. In fact two women and one man had made a serious attempt at suicide during the previous year! The psychotic group of symptoms (delusions, irrelevant speech and non-social speech, etc.) mentioned in the table related to two women who had been ill for a long time and one man who had been ill for only one year.

When the data were analysed by age group, we found that the symptom rate was lowest amongst the young, highest amongst the middle-aged, and fell slightly once again in the old age group. Only 10 per cent of those below 20 had one or more symptoms, while the rate was 40 per cent in those between 21–40, and 32 per cent in those aged 41 or above.

TABLE 6.2

Frequency of psychiatric symptoms in Sakalwada

Symptom	Frequency (%)	
	Males (N= *123*)	*Females* (N= *111*)
1. Body pain	14	14
2. Tiredness	14	6
3. Headache	4	10
4. Indigestion	7	5
5. Numbness	3	—
6. Burning sensation	1	5
7. Dizziness	2	3
8. Sleeplessness	10	8
9. Poor appetite	9	7
10. Anxiety and fear	3	3
11. Tremors	1	6
12. Palpitation	2	8
13. Sweating	2	5
14. Phobias	2	—
15. Depression	5	4
16. Dullness	3	4
17. Loss of interest	7	3
18. Suicidal ideas	4	3
19. Suicidal attempts	2	1
20. Pathological worrying	5	5
21. Irritability	10	7
22. Poor concentration	4	1
23. Restlessness	8	1
24. Subjective forgetfulness	14	5
25. Possession	2	5
26. Epileptic fits	1	—
27. Sexual problems	2	—
28. Heavy drinking	1	1
29. Delusions	1	1
30. Irrelevant speech	—	2
31. Non-social speech	—	—

The benefits of the Sakalwada study

Though the study was carried out mainly to guide us in preparing an instrument suitable for employment in a field survey, it gave us very useful insights into the way in which the villagers would receive a mental health inquiry, and practical tips about how to organise the much larger Kota survey. These may be summarised as follows:

1. There appears to be no dearth of psychiatric symptomatology in rural India, nor do the villagers find it difficult to describe their symptoms. The IPIS, which was designed to ask questions in an idiom easily understood by the illiterate villagers, of course helped to make the task of communication much easier.

2. The villagers are very willing to co-operate in a mental health inquiry if certain rules are observed:

(a) The village leaders must be seen before starting the survey. This gives them a feeling of importance, and they go out of their way to remove apprehensions amongst the other inhabitants.

(b) The women must be interviewed by women investigators. Only once did we try to find out how a woman would respond to a male investigator—but the latter was chased away by the former's father-in-law!

(c) As far as possible the males in the house should be seen before the females. They are then in a position to explain to the women the harmlessness of the inquiry.

(d) As far as possible an attempt should be made to explain the purpose of the survey to every respondent before starting the inquiry. Though the villagers do not understand the long-term benefits of research, it helps to tell them that these data will help to create a better health service in the future.

(e) Those found to be suffering from symptoms, whether psychological or physical, should be offered immediate help. Very early in the study we discovered that our prescriptions and referral letters were of little use because the villager often did not have money to buy the medicine prescribed, or to make the journey to hospital. From then onwards we started carrying with us some simple medicines for diarrhoea, worms, eye infection, etc. which we disbursed to the needy persons on the spot.

3. As far as possible the whole inquiry must be completed in one session. Very often it is difficult to trace the respondent a second time.

4. The timing of interviews must correspond with the villagers' routine. We found that the women and retired men were easily seen in their house during the day, while the working men could only be contacted in the late evening.

5. The section on 'inquiry about others' proved very useful. The psychotics and those who had attempted suicide were picked up through this section. We, however, decided that this section should be given to men only since women were reluctant to 'talk about others'. Not that they did not know about others, but they were too

much afraid of what their men might do to them if they were found to be revealing such information.

6. A team of three field investigators took about 15 days to see 234 individuals. This gave us some idea of how long it might take to complete the larger Kota survey.

7. We discovered that at least some of the items could easily be scored with confidence by the non-psychiatric members of the team. This promised the possibility of using non-psychiatrists for at least part of the interview. This assumption was tested in two reliability studies conducted with the IPSS. These are described in the next section.

The Indian Psychiatric Survey Schedule (IPSS)

This is the modified version of the IPIS, which was evolved during the Sakalwada survey. Like the IPIS, it is designed to inquire about the presence or absence of 124 psychiatric symptoms and about items of historical information. A symptom is defined as an item of behaviour, mood, speech, thinking or sensorium which (a) represents a change from the usual pattern for the individual and (b) is distressful to the subject or to those around him, or both. Unless otherwise specified the symptom is recorded if present at the time of the interview and/or during the preceding week.

The schedule was drafted in the Kannada language. An English version of the schedule, whose faithfulness to the Kannada text was checked by translation and retranslation by independent translators, is reproduced in Appendix I.

The inquiry is conducted through a multi-stage procedure:

(a) All members of the population are given the *preliminary interview schedule*. This schedule is designed for use by non-psychiatrists who have had a short period of training. It has two subsections. The first section has 26 standard questions about the subject's mental state, followed by standard supplementary questions in order to ensure that he has understood what has been asked. There are a number of cut-off points and the inquiry can be made more detailed when necessary. In this way it is possible to elicit the presence or absence of 26 'somatic' symptoms and 36 'psychological symptoms', the decision being made by the investigator guided by an instruction manual giving standard definitions for the various symptoms.

To encourage co-operation, questions are first asked about the more acceptable somatic symptoms, then about sleep, appetite and other items of subjective distress, and only at the end about delusions and hallucinations. Sub-section II has 15 questions about items of behaviour which may cause distress or embarrassment to other people; the respondent is asked whether he has observed these in any member of his family or village.

(b) Anyone who reports somatic symptoms is given a physical examination by the psychiatrist to exclude any obvious physical pathology.

(c) If fits, attempted suicide, delusions, hallucinations or possessions are suspected in the preliminary inquiry, the respondent is given a more detailed interview by a trained psychiatrist.

(d) A close relative who has been with the respondent at least one hour every day during the preceding week is given a detailed interview if:

(i) anyone while completing the Section II of the preliminary inquiry has reported that the subject suffers from one or more items in that section.

(ii) on detailed inquiry with the subject, the presence of fits, possession, delusions or hallucinations is confirmed.

(e) For every respondent who needs a detailed inquiry or whose relative is interviewed, the psychiatrist completes a schedule referring to 'observations during the interview'.

(f) When there are multiple sources of information (e.g. inquiry · from the subject, inquiry from the informant or observations during the interview) a symptom is recorded as present if it has been reported in any one of these settings.

The Sakalwada pilot survey revealed that a physical examination would be necessary in 30 per cent of the respondents, and a detailed inquiry from the respondent and/or his relative in about 5 per cent of the cases.

Training the non-medical investigators and the tests of reliability

The IPSS is based on the assumptions that a large part of the inquiry can be conducted by non-medical investigators and that they can be trained to make correct decisions about the majority of the symptoms. These assumptions were put to the test, in the following way:

A training programme was carried out at the Bangalore Mental Hospital, in which two sociologists and a psychiatric social worker were taught the use of the preliminary schedule by a trained psychiatrist. The training proceeded through the following stages:

(a) The psychiatrist interviewed 20 patients while the others watched the procedure.

(b) The psychiatrist interviewed another set of 20 patients and the trainees recorded the symptoms separately without consulting each other; subsequently their findings were compared and any areas of disagreement were reviewed.

(c) The psychiatrist and the three trainees took turns to interview 5 patients each while all four recorded symptoms for the whole group of 20 patients.

All through the training there were many discussion sessions in which the trainees put forward their doubts and queries. Also they were repeatedly tested for their knowledge of the definition of symptoms in the instruction manual.

The training was completed in three weeks and was followed by two inter-investigator reliability studies. The first study was conducted in the hospital setting with 40 patients. The psychiatrist and the three trainees examined 10 patients each, while all four recorded symptoms independently for the 40 patients. The second study was conducted in a field setting when 40 unselected members of the general population were examined in the same way as in the hospital study. Both reliability studies were limited to the preliminary interview schedule only, since the other sections were not meant for use by non-medical workers.

It was found that out of the total 2480 ratings in each study there were only 6 ratings on which the trainees disagreed amongst each other or with the psychiatrist. The disagreement, which was of similar proportion in both studies, was extremely small. It was therefore proved with overwhelming confidence that this section of the schedule could be used by non-medical investigators who had had a short period of training.

No attempt was made to conduct inter-investigator reliability checks for the other sections; these were the same as in the IPIS and their reliability had already been checked.

The IPSS was now ready for use. In the event, the same psychiatrist and the same three trainees who took part in the above-mentioned reliability studies were subsequently personally engaged in the field work of the Kota survey.

7

THE MEASUREMENT OF
SOCIAL FUNCTIONING*

One of the parameters chosen for measuring psychiatric need was that of a decline in day to day social functioning; but while designing the study we found that we ourselves were far from clear not only about the method by which this dimension would be determined empirically, but also about its very definition. It appeared that 'social functioning' and related terms could in fact be interpreted in a variety of ways, so we decided to examine various conceptual frameworks before selecting the one most relevant to the definition of psychiatric need in a non-referred population. Subsequently, we carried out two pilot studies while designing a social functioning questionnaire suitable for the Kota Survey.

In our discussions of the concept of 'level of social functioning' we soon realised that whether we considered behaviour at the top end of this scale (namely that which deploys an individual's talents to the full, in activities which are regarded as helpful to his fellows) or near the mid-point (namely behaviour which suffices to preserve the harmony of his society, or of his immediate referral group) or behaviour which is in varying degrees regarded as socially detrimental, value judgements were inescapable. Our first task, therefore, was to formulate the principal ways in which these value judgements have been applied; this led us to recognise the following models for assessing the quality of social behaviour:

The expectational model

The social functioning of an individual may be assessed from the point of view of whether he is fulfilling societal expectations. Most societies have certain minimum expectations for their members. People are expected to care for their bodily needs, dress themselves and feed themselves. In most societies, everyone has tasks which they are expected to carry out and for which they are rewarded, both materially and in terms of social esteem. In addition, people are

---

* We are indebted to Miss Dorothy Buglass of the MRC Unit for Epidemiological Studies in Psychiatry, University of Edinburgh, for much help in the clarification of concepts discussed in this chapter.

expected to refrain from certain grossly disruptive forms of behaviour; severe sanctions are almost invariably invoked against
theft, murder and rape, and in lesser degree against minor trans-
gressions against communal rules.

It is relatively easy to observe whether a person has violated the
major rules of conduct. However, if we are interested in finding
those in the society who need help and treatment, an assessment of
dysfunction which is limited to noting violations of these very basic
expectations will pick up only a very small group of seriously dysfunctioning individuals. Most clinicians would agree that many
patients who seek help and treatment, and are benefited by it, are
fulfilling these minimal expectations, but suffer or cause suffering
because they are unable to meet more subtle demands from others,
for example, from their spouse, children, parents or friends. Any
research instrument for detecting 'cases' in a population should
therefore be able to pick out this category of people also. It is, however, very difficult to lay down objective criteria for these more
complex expectations, whose fulfilment involves interpersonal per-
ceptions and demands which cannot readily be generalised. One
could adopt the approach of asking the spouse, parents, children,
etc., whether a particular person is fulfilling their respective expectations. This approach could lead to a number of difficulties. The
opinions expressed by the informants may prove contradictory, or
the informants may be influenced in their judgement by their own
psychopathology. Further, there is evidence that the relatives and
friends of the mentally sick adjust their demands according to their
experience of this person and thus make lower demands than would
other members of their community.

To sum up, assessment on the basis of minimal expectations is
insufficient; objective criteria cannot be laid down for the more
subtle expectations of relatives and friends, and direct inquiry from
the relatives and friends may give conflicting, unreliable and often
invalid information.

The ideal model

The concept of ideal social functioning is the social equivalent of
'positive mental health'. It presupposes that a given society prescribes the kind of conduct which is desirable for its members in
particular areas of living. It can be viewed as the opposite end of the
continuum from the 'minimal expectations'. Whereas the criterion
of minimal expectation identifies only those who are severely dysfunctioning, the concept of ideal functioning provides a framework
within which all individuals of the society can be judged and ranked

according to how closely their behaviour approximates to the pre-scribed ideal standards.

It is very difficult to use this model for empirical assessment of individuals' behaviour. It is true that different societies do subscribe to social philosophies which influence people's behaviour. These philosophies, however, lay down general rather than specific lines of conduct. Further, many of these precepts contain elements of contradiction. Even if the contradictions are accepted, the relative importance of different components remains ambiguous. For example, a Christian is expected both to be charitable to his enemies and to fight against injustice. How unjust must his enemies be before he ceases to be charitable? Again, what is 'good' according to the tenets of a particular philosophy is assessed on multidutinous variables which are not additive in any simple fashion. Thus, the relative merits of the conduct of different individuals cannot easily be assessed.

For all these reasons, an 'ideal' model seems unsuitable for empirical assessment of individuals' social functioning.

The 'social contribution' model

Social functioning may be viewed from the angle of a person's contribution to the 'good' of the society at large. A person's contribution, however, depends very much on his occupation, and it is difficult to determine the relative merits of various occupations. It is true that some occupations (such as the practice of medicine) are considered more beneficial, are more highly valued and given higher status than many others, but the latter, the less valued occupations (such as those of the sanitary engineer or the dustman), may in fact be no less essential for the proper functioning of the society. It would be naive to say that a person is functioning less well because he belongs to a less highly valued occupation. Some social analysts have argued that an individual's worth may be assessed by determining how well he fulfills his 'own potential' in his particular occupation. In terms of empirical application, this adds a second unquantifiable variable, namely 'potential' to the already highly complex one, 'societal need'. In short, the social contribution model, too, seems unsuitable for determining the social functioning of an individual.

The average model

According to this model, social dysfunction consists in behaving differently from other people. In its simplest form this approach would consist in evaluating the performance of a large number of individuals in a society on certain selected items of behaviour, establishing the observed norms, and considering as dysfunctioning those who fall a given distance away from the mean. The main problem arises in choosing the relevant items of behaviour, for which norms are to be established. It is obvious that decisions about relevant items cannot be left to the investigator, who will be influenced in his choice by the social values of his own referral group. The relevance of the items must be determined on the basis of the expectations and values of the members of the society in question. Mention may be made here of a study carried out by Hogarty and Katz (1970), who found that statistical norms on certain selected items of behaviour differed in a group of 450 normals according to age, civil state and social class. Younger people, the widowed and those in lower social classes scored lower on their scales than the older, the married and those of higher social class. This may be due to the fact that the norms of performance really were low in the former groups; but there is also the alternative explanation that while they did not perform the activities included in the scales used, they performed instead certain other alternative activities which were not inquired about.

This shows that, while the performance of certain specified items of behaviour can be observed and quantified, the interpretation of such findings calls for a study of the expectations and values of the society as a whole, and also of various subgroups within the society. These are major undertakings in themselves.

The historical model

The social functioning of an individual can be assessed by comparing his present performance on selected items of behaviour with his previous performance. Clinicians often make this comparison when determining the seriousness of an individual's illness. Once again the problem consists in deciding which items of behaviour shoud be chosen for determining the present and past performances of the individual. Secondly, very often epidemiological studies are cross-sectional, and it is difficult to place reliance on information about past performance whether given by the person himself or by those close to him.

The Kota social functioning questionnaire

For the Kota inquiry we wanted to develop an instrument which would take into account the value orientation of the society being investigated rather than that of the investigator. Further, we wanted the assessment to be based on verifiable concrete units of behaviour rather than on qualitative subjective impressions of the respondent or the informants. Finally, we wished the inquiry to be structured and yet to include a sufficiently wide range of items to ensure that those picked out as dysfunctioning would not consist only of the very severely disturbed.

In the preceding sections, we have already rejected the 'ideal' and the 'social contribution' models as too heterogeneous and complex for use in population studies. In the Kota Study, we adopted an approach which may be described as a modification of the 'expectational' model. We set out to collect, as a first step, those items of behaviour which the 'group' *expected* in the day to day functioning of its members, and then, as a second step, we retained in our questionnaire only those items which in fact were reported by the majority of our respondents. We did this because some respondents tend to describe expectations which prove to be purely ideal, and unrelated to actual performance; we wanted the questionnaire to assess only realistic expectations.

In practice the design of our questionnaire was accomplished through two pilot studies. First, we inquired from three unselected members of each caste and sex group* what kind of behaviour they expected from a male and a female respectively in the areas of (a) work, (b) leisure, (c) husband-wife relationship, (d) parent-child relationships, and (e) religious activities. The interview was purely unstructured except when the respondents lapsed into an adjectival description of their expectations. For example, when they said that the husband should be good to his wife, we asked them to describe what the husband should do to be seen as 'good'. When they said that men should work hard, we asked them to describe what working 'hard' meant in terms of hours per day, number of occupations, contribution to the tasks at home, or working during the slack monsoon season, etc.

A comprehensive list of items of behaviour in each area was prepared from these interviews. Knowing that these expectations might be too high, we carried out a second pilot study to inquire how often these expectations were actually met in practice. Adopting a quota sampling procedure, we gave a questionnaire based on the collected items to five members of each caste, age and sex group,† asking each respondent to state how often, if at all, they practised the given item of behaviour.

An analysis was carried out and we found that the different caste,

---

* There were 18 respondents in this study.

† There were three castes, two sexes and four age groups (15–20, 21–40, 41–60, and 61 +). Thus, there were 120 respondents in this exercise.

sex and age groups differed in their practice of the expected behaviours.

We found, for example, that the Brahmin men helped their wives in home tasks (sweeping, cleaning, watering the vegetable garden, etc.) more often than did the Bants and Mogers. They also claimed to visit their friends and relatives much more often than the other two groups. More than half of the Mogers claimed to spend at least two evenings a week in the local drink-shop as compared with only 20 per cent of the Bants. More than 90 per cent of the Mogers claimed that they gave money for personal expenditure to their wives, as compared with only 60 per cent of Bants and 50 per cent of the Brahmins. Many more of the Mogers claimed that they took their wives out for entertainment at least once a week, compared to the Brahmins and Bants.

Brahmin women reported going to temples and Bhutasthanas much more frequently than did Bant and Moger women. They also visited their parents much more often than did the Bant and Moger women.

It was found that the young men went to entertainments much more often than the middle-aged and old, but drank much less than the other groups. The middle-aged visited temples and helped in the household tasks more often than either the young or the old.

Our hope was to prepare 'norms' for the population against which the functioning of those with psychiatric symptoms might be evaluated. However, when we found consistent differences in behaviour in the different caste, age and sex groups, we realised that norms would be necessary for each of the subgroups. Again, since functioning might also depend on education and income level, the number of subgroups for which norms would be necessary was expected to be more than a hundred! Considering that data would be required on at least 30 members in each subgroup, in order to work out reliable means and standard deviations, the task appeared to be stupendous—far beyond the scope of the present study.

We decided to give up our hope of preparing community-wide norms, and to content ourselves with within-group comparisons of those with and without symptoms. However, we achieved our objective of keeping only the 'realistic' expectations by including in our final questionnaire only those items which were practised by at least half of the respondents in the second pilot study. We also omitted such items as were ambiguous, produced unreliable and contradictory answers, were of poor discriminatory ability, or were characteristic of one caste, or one age group only.

This exercise robbed the original draft schedule of the majority of its items. Such was the variability of behaviour amongst members of the different groups, and even amongst the members of the same group, that the total number of items which were practised by more than 50 per cent of the population was very small and did not really test more than minimal social expectations. Having started with a desire to go beyond the examination of minimal expectations, to find that we had returned to this same point after a great amount of hard thinking and hard work was a sobering experience indeed!

The one advantage that this denuded questionnaire still-possessed was that it contained concrete items which were derived from actual behaviour of the representatives of the population to be examined and hence were more applicable to the local context than those belonging to a questionnaire developed in another social context might have been. The questionnaire is reproduced in Appendix II.

The items were grouped into six categories: (1) work, (2) entertainment, (3) visits to relatives and friends, (4) religious activities, (5) sexual functioning (frequency of sexual intercourse) and (6) time spent with children in the evening. The questions in category 5 were limited to married men below the age of 50, and those in category 6 to married men who had one or more children of their own. Women were not asked category 5 questions because they were too bashful, nor category 6 questions because they all claimed to spend time with their children in the evening. A peculiar difficulty was experienced in respect of men's work. It was very difficult to separate 'good' from 'bad' workers from the number of hours spent in the field or at sea since, firstly, they were too hazy in their estimates of the number of hours, and secondly the mere number of hours gives no guide to the quality of their work. The number of hours worked did, however, provide quite a useful guide during the rainy season, which is a period of rest and during which some of the villagers simply laze around without any fear of being condemned for this. There are, however, a number of persons who spend a few hours each day on jobs which earn them some money, and they are quite clear about the number of hours they devote to such activity. The fact that the questionnaire was used subsequently during the rainy season helped a lot—the number of hours the people put in did not have to be recalled from memory of events some months earlier. The performance of work during the slack rainy season was taken as an indicator of each man's work in general.

The scoring procedure for individual ratings was based on whether a particular activity was performed at all and, if 'yes', how often. For example, in the case of women's 'work' a score of '1' was given if a particular activity (e.g. cooking vegetables) was performed three or four times a week, and a score of '3' if it was performed five or more times a week. A score of 'o' was given if the activity was not performed at all. The scores on various items in one category were combined. For women's 'work', which had six items, a person could therefore score from 'o' to '18'.

It was difficult to decide whether the scores in different categories should be combined and, if so, how the categories should be weighted with respect to each other. For example, should a person who does no work but scores high on entertainment and religious activities get as much credit as one who works a lot but gets low score in other categories? A subsequent exercise showed that the scores in different categories were very poorly and inconsistently correlated—it was decided, therefore, to evaluate performance in different categories separately.

As we have mentioned earlier, the idea of developing 'objective' norms of functioning was dropped because of the complexity of the task. As it turned out, respondents with symptoms showed no difference in social functioning scores from those without symptoms; hence social functioning as measured by this questionnaire was not therefore included in our eventual measurements of need, which are described in Chapter 12.

8

THE SURVEY OF MENTAL DISORDER

The study of Kota and its people, the exploration of the existing health care system, the preparation of the IPSS and that of the social functioning questionnaire—enlightening as these exercises were in their own right—were only preparatory groundwork. The comparative study of mental disorder amongst the Brahmins, Bants and Mogers was the main focus of our investigation, and this was carried out during July to October 1972. The timing of the survey was deliberate: during these months of heavy rains both agricultural work and fishing come to a halt, and people are not too busy to answer questions.

The sampling procedure

Because of the practical limitations set by the size of the investigating team and the time at our disposal, we decided to restrict our study to a 50 per cent sample of the adults in each caste group, an adult being defined as anyone who at the time of inquiry was aged 15 years or more. Instead of taking the sample at random, we adopted the procedure of first selecting a geographical area which promised to have within its bounds 50 per cent of the *families* of each caste group, and then including in the sample all the adults from these families.

For the purposes of the electoral register the Kota village is divided into 62 geographical units called 'Bettus'. The 1970 census records were examined and such 13 Bettus were taken as came nearest to the criterion of having 50 per cent of the Brahmin, Bant and Moger families respectively. Table 8.1 compares the distribution of the families in the whole village and that in the 13 Bettus (hereafter referred to as the sample area).

Table 8.2 compares the distribution of the individual *adults* in the whole village and in the sample area. The comparison is limited to the members of the three castes only. It is apparent that the proportion of the Brahmins in the sample (56 per cent) is more than that originally planned, but the discrepancy was not significant. This slight disproportion in the sample was more than compensated by three major advantages bestowed by this particular sampling procedure: firstly, by reducing the total number of Bettus from 62 to

TABLE 8.1

**Distribution of the Brahmin, Bant and Moger families
in the whole village and in the sample area**

	Number of families		
	Brahmins	Bants	Mogers
Whole village	256	112	302
Sample area	128	61	155
Percentage of the total in the sample area	50%	54%	51%

TABLE 8.2

**Distribution of the Brahmin, Bant and Moger adults
in the whole village and the sample area**

	Number of adults		
	Brahmins	Bants	Mogers
Whole village	972	449	1255
Sample area	556	233	623
Percentage of the total in the sample area	56%	49%	50%

13, the procedure helped greatly in minimising the daily walking distance. This made it possible to complete the survey in much shorter time than would have been necessary to screen individual respondents spread at random throughout the village area. Secondly, since complete geographical units were taken, it was possible to observe whether people who lived near to each other suffered from similar types of symptoms; and thirdly, since complete family units were taken, it was possible to determine whether certain families had a higher symptom rate than others. Answers to these questions are of obvious interest to students of psychiatric epidemiology.

The instruments of inquiry

The instruments employed were the Indian Psychiatric Survey Schedule (IPSS), the social functioning questionnaire, and a short questionnaire inquiring about a few selected, operationally defined socio-demographic variables. They were used in the following manner:

1. All respondents were given the IPSS and the questionnaire about socio-demographic variables.

2. Every one reporting one or more symptoms on the IPSS was given the social functioning questionnaire and also asked whether,

because of these symptoms, he or she found it difficult to cope with day to day work and social relations.

3. The social functioning questionnaire was also given to every second male and every third female without symptoms. Data about the social functioning of the psychiatrically normal was obviously necessary for any comparative analysis, but restricting the questioning to only a sample of the normals saved much valuable time.

The operational procedure

The investigation was carried out by a team of one psychiatrist and three non-medical research investigators who had been trained to use the IPSS. The team was directly supervised, throughout the survey, by Dr Kapur, and assisted by Mr Guruva Markala, a local guide.

Before launching the main survey, a pilot survey was carried out with 100 men and women from the non-sample area (data on 40 of these was used for the 'field' reliability study mentioned in Chapter 6). This pilot study, which lasted about 20 days, provided the following benefits:

1. It helped the investigators to learn the correct technique of asking questions, especially of the respondents who had no obvious symptoms.

2. It gave us the opportunity to reconstruct some of the questions in the local idiom.

3. It taught us that the interview would take 15–20 minutes on an average, that the psychiatrist would be called to give a physical examination to roughly 25–30 per cent of the respondents, and that a detailed interview would be required for only about 5 per cent of the respondents. We also learnt that the team, working 7–8 hours a day, would be able to see roughly 20 cases each day. This knowledge was of great advantage in planning the course and duration of the study.

4. The villagers (even those in the sample area) came to know about our investigation and were prepared for us when we went to them. They learnt that the questioning was not prolonged and that the team gave free medicines when required. This advance publicity about the nature of our work helped greatly in getting co-operation during the main survey.

The main survey

Our plan was to complete 20 interviews a day, and to complete the interviews in one Bettu before proceeding to the next. We started in the coastal area and gradually worked our way inland. Armed with our map of the village and heralded by the guide

Guruva (who, being a local folk-drama artiste, was well known amongst the villagers), the team moved from house to house, starting every day at 9 a.m. and finishing by 5 p.m. or so. Miss Kshama and Miss Lalitha would see the women, Mr Eshwar would see the men, and Dr Sayeed would give the physical examination and the detailed interview whenever called upon to do so. Since Dr Sayeed was on the spot all the time, it was not necessary to leave the detailed investigation till later—something we had found very inconvenient during the Sakalwada Survey. Though our aim was to complete 20 interviews a day, we were frequently able to do more. Whenever possible the interview was carried out in privacy, but often we had to see men while they were working in their vegetable gardens or mending their fishing-nets, and women while they were engaged in cooking or cleaning the house. Our Sakalwada experience had taught us not to insist on formality, so we often spent a little time discussing the respondent's work or current village gossip. The team members did not flinch from sitting down on the unclean floors or accepting offers of drinks in dirty cups. This behaviour often excited complimentary remarks from the villagers, to the effect that we were 'not spoilt by the city life'!

The villagers knew that we would give medicines when required. The medicines most in demand were those for diarrhoea, worms, anaemia and scabies. What really turned the tide in our favour was the successful treatment of a few epileptics who had had frequent fits for years. One particular epileptic decided to join our daily rounds and thus acted as a walking symbol of our good faith.

A necessary part of our daily routine was the 'evening meeting' when the members of the team would sit with Dr Kapur, go through the day's work, tick off from the master list those who had been seen during the day, and clarify any items about which they had been uncertain.

After completing one Bettu we would go through it once again with a view to interviewing those who had been missed at the first visit. In spite of this, we found that when we completed one full round of the sample area in $2\frac{1}{2}$ months, about 200 respondents had been left out for a variety of reasons. This necessitated yet another round which occupied another 15 days.

During the survey we discovered that some of the individuals in the 1970 census list had died and some others had left the village. Also, a few had come to reside in the sample area permanently. It was decided not to pursue those who had left the village but to include in the sample those who had come in since 1970. Table 8.3 shows the new adjusted figures.

TABLE 8.3

Adult Brahmins, Bants and Mogers who had died, left the village or moved in since 1970 census

	1970 figures	Died	Left	Moved in	1972 figures
Brahmins	556	86	13	19	476
Bants	233	38	3	12	204
Mogers	623	41	18	45	609
Total	1412	165	34	76	1289

We were therefore expected to interview 1289 respondents. It was, however, discovered that 48 individuals, though counted as permanent residents of the village, were away from it throughout the survey period. These could not be interviewed, nor could a total of 8 (4 males, 4 females) who were at home but refused to co-operate in the inquiry. Table 8.4 shows the total number of people in each caste interviewed during the survey.

TABLE 8.4

Men and women interviewed

	Male	Female	Total
Brahmins	154	299	453
Bants	55	143	198
Mogers	217	365	582
Total	426	807	1233

Out of the possible 1289 respondents, 1233 were interviewed. This gave a response rate of 96 per cent. However, if we do not include those 48 who were unavailable because of being temporarily away from home (and who might have co-operated had they been in the village), the response rate works out to be more than 99 per cent.

9

PSYCHIATRIC SYMPTOMS AND
THEIR CORRELATES

It is well worth recapitulating that in this study we had renounced
the desire of categorising psychiatric morbidity under diagnostic
labels and had chosen instead a simpler but in the event much more
reliable estimate of mental disorder—psychiatric symptoms. This
chapter describes the distribution of these symptoms and examines
certain socio-demographic correlates which might be of aetiological
significance.

Though only half of the adult Brahmins, Bants and Mogers were
interviewed, there is no reason to believe that these people were in
any way unique and different from other adult members of the three
castes who were not included in the sample. A comparison of the
sample group with the others on sex, age, education and income
distribution did not reveal any statistically significant differences.

It is true that forty-eight people who should have been interviewed
were not in fact seen as they were away temporarily on road building
projects. This temporary migration occurs every year during the
monsoon season and there is no reason to suspect that those who
were away differed in psychiatric morbidity from those in station.
Another eight refused to co-operate. Their mental health was
assessed as far as possible by making inquiries from their family
members and neighbours. They were reported to be symptom free.
It must be stressed that the combined non-response rate is in any
case too low (4 per cent) to bias the results in any serious manner.

The main purpose of the inquiry was to make comparisons
among the three castes. Because of differences in the data collection
procedures and in the criteria for ascertaining psychiatric morbidity,
the results in this study cannot be strictly compared with those
obtained in other studies carried out in India or abroad. Only
general statements can be made about any striking differences or
similarities.

In this chapter and those which follow, the symptoms are categorised in a variety of ways, each regarded as most suitable for the
analysis being undertaken or for illustrating a particular argument.
For example, at times we have defined anyone with one or more
symptoms as a 'case', and at others we have grouped the respondents

according to the type or number of symptoms. None of these classifications is considered to be final or 'better' than the others.

The socio-demographic correlates of symptoms

An analysis was carried out to see whether there were any sex differences in symptom rates and whether age, education, income, occupation, marital status and type of family were in any way related to having symptoms or not. For this series of analyses any one with one or more symptoms was considered to be a psychiatric 'case'. Statistical tests (X^2 test) were carried out to compare the 'case' rates in each of the sex, age, education, income, occupation, marital status and family type categories, and differences were accepted or significant only if the probability of the null hypothesis being true was less than ·05. For the sake of simplicity of presentation the tables show only the total number of respondents and the case rate in each category. The percentages are rounded off to the nearest whole number. The actual X^2 values are not shown but the probability of the null hypothesis' being correct is given in the text.

Out of the 1233 respondents interviewed 456 had one or more psychiatric symptoms. The 'case' rate in the total group therefore was 37 per cent.

1. *Sex:* An analysis was carried out to see if the 'case' rate differed amongst men and women. 32 per cent of men and 40 per cent of women were found to have one or more sypmtoms (Table 9.1). This difference was statistically significant at $p < ·01$.

TABLE 9.1

Sex differences and the 'case' rate

	Males (426)	Females (807)
Number of 'cases'	135	321
'Case' rate	32%	40%

The rest of the analyses were carried out separately for men and women.

2. *Age:* The respondents, both males and females, were divided into six age categories: 15–20, 21–30, 31–40, 41–50, 51–60 and 61 or more. The 'case' rates in these age categories were compared (Table 9.2). It can be seen that the 'case' rate rises sharply till the age if 40, after which there is hardly any rise. This is true for males and females. The differences in the six age categories are statistically significant at $p < ·001$ both for males and females. It can be seen that the females have a higher 'case' rate than males in each age category.

TABLE 9.2

Age differences and 'case' rate

		15–20	21–20	31–40	41–50	51–60	61 +
Males:	Total	(72)	(88)	(88)	(70)	(55)	(53)
	'Case' rate	12%	20%	36%	43%	40%	45%
Females:	Total	(187)	(184)	(148)	(111)	(81)	(96)
	'Case' rate	20%	31%	42%	55%	56%	56%

3. *Education:* Those with primary education or less were compared with those who had had higher education. It was found that those with higher education had a much smaller 'case' rate than those with low education. (Males: low education—38 per cent; higher education—18 per cent. Females: low education—43 per cent; higher education—22 per cent.) This was of course to be expected. Higher education having become popular only recently in the last two decades or so, the high education group would have a greater proportion of young people than the low education group—and it had already been shown that the young people have a lower 'case' rate. To remove this bias from the analysis a comparison was made separately for those aged 15–20 and those aged 21–40. (The numbers of those with higher education in above 40 age groups were too small for statistical purposes.) It was shown that while there was hardly any difference in the 'case' rates amongst the more or less educated respondents in the 15–20 age group, in those between 21–40, the 'low education' group had a much higher 'case' rate than in the 'high education' group. This was true both for males and females and the differences were statistically significant in each case at $p < \cdot 05$. The results are shown in Table 9.3.

TABLE 9.3

Education and 'case' rate

	Males 15–20		Males 21–20	
	Low education (22)	Higher education (50)	Low education (128)	Higher education (48)
'Case' rate	14%	12%	33%	17%

	Females 15–20		Females 21–40	
	Low education (103)	Higher education (84)	Low education (290)	Higher education (42)
'Case' rate	21%	19%	38%	28%

4. *Income:* Respondents were divided into three income groups: Poor (per capita incomes up to Rs. 200 per annum); Average (per capita incomes of Rs. 201–Rs. 800 per annum), and Comfortable (per capita incomes over Rs. 800 per annum). The 'case' rates in the three groups were compared separately for males and females. As is shown in Table 9.4 the poor males have a much higher 'case' rate than the average or comfortable males but amongst females there is hardly any difference between the three groups. The differences in the case of males were statistically significant at $p < .05$.

TABLE 9.4

Income and 'case' rate

		Poor	Average	Comfortable
Males:	Total	(42)	(271)	(113)
	'Case' rate	47%	30%	30%
Females:	Total	(146)	(532)	(129)
	'Case' rate	41%	40%	40%

5. *Occupation:* Men whose main occupation was farming were compared with those with fishing, business and service as their main occupations. No statistically significant differences were observed. Since occupation is often related to income and the poor had been shown to have a higher case rate, comparisons were carried out separately for the three income categories. Once again no statistically significant differences were observed.

Those men who were employed in any occupation were compared with those claiming to have no work. Students were excluded from this analysis.

The unemployed were found to have a much higher 'case' rate (56 per cent) than those who had some occupation (31 per cent). The differences are statistically significant at $p < .05$.

6. *Marital status:* The unmarried, the married and the widowed were compared for 'case' rates. Since age is related to marital status and the different age categories had already been found to have different 'case' rates this comparison was controlled for age. There were few married or widowed persons among the 15–20 age group, so no analysis was carried out for this group. Those aged 21–40 included very few who were widowed, so for them comparisons were made only between the married and the unmarried. Those aged 41 or above included very few 'unmarried' so in this group comparisons were made only between the married and the widowed.

No differences in 'case' rates were observed between the married and the unmarried aged between 21–40, both males and females.

When comparison was carried out between the married and widowed aged 41 or more, there was a trend towards the widowed of both sexes having a higher 'case' rate than the married; the differences, however, failed to reach statistical significance.

7. *Family:* Those living in a joint family setting were compared with those living in a unitary family setting. The 'case' rates were almost identical in the two groups. (Males: joint family—33 per cent; unitary family—31 per cent; Females: joint family—40 per cent; unitary family—40 per cent.)

An analysis was carried out to see whether the family setting might have a different relation to 'case' rates in the different age, education and income categories. No such differences were observed. Comparisons were carried out separately for the married and unmarried. Again no differences were observed.

An analysis was carried out to see whether the size of the family was related to 'case' rates. When these rates were compared for people from family size: less than 5, 6–10, 11–15 and 16 or more, no differences were seen.

Some comments on the socio-demographic correlates

The above analyses were carried out in order to identify any socio-demographic correlates of sub-groups with high or low 'case' rates, so that any inter-caste differences in 'case' rates could be properly interpreted. The results are, however, interesting in their own right.

1. The sex differences, with females having a higher 'case' rate, are in accordance with the results obtained in most epidemiological studies across the world. Such a result could not, however, be confidently expected if one were to look at the busy psychiatric outpatient clinics in India or at the records of Indian mental hospitals, where the men greatly outnumber the women. Many hospital-based or out-patient clinic-based studies in India (e.g. Neki and Kapur, 1963) demonstrate a preponderance of men. It may be argued that in a field survey women more readily complain of symptoms which in fact are not serious enough to require help, and that their being in a minority in counts of attendance at the hospital is an indication that they have fewer serious symptoms than do men. In this study a 'need assessment' was made and therefore it was possible to examine this hypothesis. The results, given in Chapter 12, do not support the above hypothesis.

2. The fact that the case rate rises with age is also in accordance with results obtained in other epidemiological studies. It is interesting, however, to note that there is very little increase after the age of

40. If one infers that the rise in 'case' rate with age represents the toll taken by accumulating life stresses, then why is there no further increase after 40? Is there less stress after this age? One is tempted to hypothesise that in the Indian culture where old people are looked after by their children and have very few responsibilities, life after 40 is perhaps less stressful. In order to test this hypothesis we compared the old people living in Joint families with those living in Unitary families. We thought that the latter would probably continue to have responsibilities and would show a higher 'case' rate compared with those in the Joint families—but this plausible hypothesis was not confirmed either for the men, or for the women.

3. The fact that poor education is related to higher 'case' rates only in the older age group may mean that the differences start being felt only after the age of 20 when a poor education might come in the way of achieving various satisfactions in later life.

4. The fact that poverty is related to higher case rates only in men might mean that the women who are not in fact responsible for being the breadwinners might feel comparitively less frustrated when there is a lack of money.

5. It is interesting that in this study family type (Joint vs Unitary) was not significantly related to case rate.

Two studies from India have conclusively shown that Joint families have a higher case rate than the Unitary families (Dube 1971 and Thakore 1974). We submit that the method of analysis is erroneous in both the studies. Case rates are worked out in both the studies from the number of families, and not from the *number of people* in those families. A joint family being larger has a greater probability of having a 'case' and hence a few Joint families would show more cases while the Unitary families would have to be more numerous, in order to provide an equal number of persons at risk.

6. Dube's study has also shown that the unemployed have a higher case rate compared with the employed and he ascribes the difference to unemployment stress. Similar results are seen in this study. The results can, however, also be interpreted to mean that persons who report symptoms may, because of illness, be more likely to be unemployed as compared with the symptom-free.

Caste and symptom rate

An analysis was next carried out to see whether the proportions of those with one or more symptoms differed in the members of the three caste groups. The results are shown in Table 9.5.

In both males and females the Brahmins have the lowest 'case' rate and the Bants have the highest 'case' rate. The male Mogers do

TABLE 9.5

'Case' rates in the three caste groups

		Brahmins	Bants	Mogers
Males:	Total	(154)	(55)	(217)
	'Case' rate	29%	39%	32%
Females:	Total	(299)	(143)	(365)
	'Case' rate	33%	43%	42%

not differ very much from the male Brahmins, and the 'case' rate in female Mogers is almost identical with that of the female Bants. The differences across the three castes in both males and females are statistically significant at $p < .05$.

It can be claimed that the low case rate in the Brahmins could be due to their having a higher proportion of the young, educated and high income members, each of those factors having already been found to be correlated with low 'case' rates. The differences on those variables between the Brahmins and the other caste groups were not, however, found to be statistically significant. Still, an attempt was made to analyse the differences in 'case' rate amongst the three caste groups, controlling one at a time for age, education and income variables. It was found that though often the numbers in some of the cells were too small for statistical analysis, the trend towards the Brahmins having the lowest 'case' rate and the Bants having the highest 'case' rate was maintained in all the analyses.

What do these differences mean? Do the Bants really have a higher mental morbidity that the other groups? This question cannot be answered from the 'case' rate alone. It would be necessary to examine the nature of symptoms reported by the three groups to see whether the Bants report greater inability to cope with demands of life, whether they consult more and whether they exhibit a greater degree of social dysfunctioning. These questions are tackled in the subsequent chapters.

Social change in the matrilineal castes and 'the case' rate

One of the most significant stresses in the matrilineal castes, reported in the earlier chapters, is the change from a traditionally matrilineal pattern of residence to a patrilineal system of living (page 33). Villagers had told us that this change often resulted in unfamiliar and unsatisfactory patterns of domestic life which were stressful to the members of the community, especially the women.

An analysis was carried out to see whether those married Bants and Mogers who still continued to reside in the traditional manner (i.e. women continuing to live in their parents' house after marriage) differed in 'case' rates from those who had changed over completely to a patrilineal system of residence or who were still in the process of transition. Subjective reports were cross-checked with objective facts, and only those respondents were accepted as having 'changed over', whose living pattern had followed the patrilineal model for at least nine months out of the previous one year. The results are shown in Table 9·6.

TABLE 9.6

Residence patterns and 'case' rates among formerly matrilineal spouses

		Pattern of residence	
		Traditional	Changed over
Males:	Total	(113)	(93)
	'Case' rate	32%	38%
Females:	Total	(222)	(115)
	'Case' rate	36%	55%

There is a trend towards both males and females who had 'changed over' showing a higher case rate compared with those who continued to live in the traditional manner but the differences were statistically significant only in the case of females ($p < ·05$).

The comparison was repeated separately for the Bant and Moger women and in both cases the women who had changed over had a higher 'case' rate (Bants: Traditional—26 per cent; Changed over—47 per cent; Mogers: Traditional—39 per cent; Changed over—55 per cent).

In any attempt to prove conclusively that social change is conducive to an increase in mental disorder it is necessary to show that the change preceded the increase and not vice versa. To accomplish this it is necessary to conduct a prospective study which is not only difficult but has its own problems, for example in ensuring the sameness of criteria for recording mental disorder at different points in time.

In considering the possible relationship between changes in residence patterns, and increased frequency of symptoms in the women involved, the following observations can be made:

1. The social change can definitely be ascribed to legal changes in the country, and any conjecture that the change in living patterns might be the result of neurosis in females has to be dismissed.

2. The decision as to place of residence in every case was made by men, and women had no say in the matter.

3. Women had in fact something to lose in terms of status by the change-over, and it cannot be argued that neurotic women would force such a change by pressurising their husbands.

There is therefore sufficient circumstantial evidence that this social change has led to an increase in mental disorder in the Bant and Moger women.

THE PATTERNS OF PSYCHIATRIC
SYMPTOMS

In the previous chapter a 'case' was defined as anyone with one or more symptoms. It was convenient to use such a definition because, if we had tried to find the socio-demographic correlates of individual symptoms, more often than not we would have had too few 'cases' for the purposes of statistical analysis. Symptoms are, however, not all alike, and different symptoms can tell a different story about the individuals or groups under consideration. In this chapter an attempt is made to explore the variety of symptoms reported by the respondents.

First of all, we present in Table 10.1 the rate of occurrence of the twelve major categories of symptoms in the entire sample (IPSS

TABLE 10.1

Distribution of symptom categories

	Males		Females		Total	
	No.	%	No.	%	No.	%
1. Somatic sensory symptoms	55	13	195	24	250	20
2. Other somatic symptoms	42	10	169	21	211	17
3. Sleeplessness	50	12	117	15	167	14
4. Forgetfulness and poor concentration	40	9	103	13	143	112
5. Irritability and tensions	19	5	46	6	65	5
6. Anxiety and worries	11	3	30	4	41	3
7. Depressive symptoms	17	4	21	3	38	3
8. Possessions and hysterical fits	8	2	26	3	34	3
9. Psychotic symptoms	11	3	5	1	16	1
10. Epileptic fits	3	1	4	1	7	1
11. Mental retardation	3	1	3	1	6	1
12. Alcoholism	5	1	—	—	5	1

did not have any specific questions regarding mental retardation; respondents were included in the category on the basis of history of inability to learn or having been backward from early childhood).

Each of these categories groups together those symptoms (out of the 124 listed in our Survey Schedule) which appear to be more similar to each other than to the others. To be included in a category, a respondent needed to have one or more symptoms of that particular group, not necessarily all such symptoms. The categories in Table 10.1 are overlapping, that is to say a person having symptoms pertaining to more than one category is counted, for calculation of rates, in each of the respective categories. For the purpose of subsequent analyses, we also grouped the respondents who reported symptoms in three additional ways, as follows:

Second method of grouping

The respondents were divided into four groups: (1) Those with no symptoms—68 per cent of the men, 60 per cent of the women; (2) those with somatic symptoms only—7 per cent of the men, 12 per cent of the women; (3) those with psychological symptoms only—15 per cent of the men, 10 per cent of the women; and (4) those with both somatic and psychological symptoms—10 per cent of the men, 18 per cent of the women. 'Somatic' symptoms include headaches, vague bodily pains, burning, itching, weakness, indigestion and nausea, while the term 'psychological' refers to symptoms in all other categories. These terms are used for convenience only and it should not be inferred that somatic symptoms are not of psychological origin.

Third method of grouping

A hierarchical classification of symptoms was carried out. In this procedure each person was assigned to the class associated with his or her highest-ranking symptom and was excluded from the lower classes even if he also had symptoms pertaining to the latter. The results according to this grouping procedure are given in Table 10.2.

It must be admitted that this hierarchical classification looks like a backdoor approach to diagnostic labelling, which we have condemned! Unreliable as the diagnostic process is, it often helps the clinician to decide on the prognosis and the line of treatment. For example, a diagnosis of psychosis indicates a different line of treatment from that of neurosis. With this in view we decided to group the individuals with one or more symptoms in a few mutually exclusive categories which would be easy to identify, relatively uncontroversial, and of some value in deciding the prognosis and course of treatment. The difficulty, of course, is that in any such classification a person may have symptoms pertaining to more than one category, and it is difficult to decide in which group to include

TABLE 10.2

Hierarchical classification of symptoms

	Males (426)		Females (807)		Total (1233)	
	No.	%	*No.*	%	*No.*	%
1. Epilepsy	3	1	4	1	7	1
2. Psychosis	10	2	3	1	13	1
3. Depression	17	4	21	3	38	3
4. Anxieties and worries	5	1	8	1	13	1
5. Other neurotic symptoms*	64	14	167	20	231	18
6. Possession states + hysteria	7	2	23	3	30	3
7. Somatic symptoms	29	7	94	11	123	10
8. No symptoms	291	68	487	60	778	63

*Subjective forgetfulness, poor concentration, muscular tension, restlessness, irritability.

him. We decided to include such a person in the category indicated by the highest-ranked of his or her symptoms. The hierarchy itself was constructed by allotting that symptom group the first position which in our opinion gave the firmest indication as to the line of treatment and prognosis, and so on down the line.

An examination of Table 10.2 will show that epilepsy has been given the top place in the hierarchy. This is because a person who has epileptic fits must first be treated for the relief of such fits; treatment of any accompanying psychotic or neurotic features is secondary. A psychotic must first have treatment for the relief of the psychotic symptoms and the treatment of any accompanying 'neurotic' features takes second place. Within the neurotic group the treatment of depressive symptoms appears to us to be more urgent than that of anxiety. Symptoms like tension, restlessness, forgetfulness, irritability and poor concentration were grouped together because we could not say which of them merited priority in terms of treatment or prognosis. 'Possession state' in the absence of psychotic or neurotic features came next because we were less confident in categorising this as a psychiatric disorder than was the case in the other categories. For the same reason somatic symptoms were ranked lowest, next to 'no symptoms'.

It is not difficult to criticise this hierarchy. There may be particular instances in which a person with neurotic symptoms has a more urgent need for treatment than one with psychotic symptoms. To those who criticise our scheme, we have this defence to offer:

(a) we consider this as only one of the ways of grouping symptoms; (b) since the criteria for ascertaining symptoms, grouping them and giving the groups a place in the hierarchy are operationally defined, this appears a better method of consolidating information for the purpose of research than the use of diagnostic labels based largely on clinical intuition; (c) finally, this hierarchy made it possible for us to seek correlation between social functioning, consultation and psychiatric need and membership of these different symptom groups, which would not have been possible if we had used the classification given in Table 10.1, in which the categories were overlapping.

Fourth method of grouping

We also grouped our respondents according to the number of symptoms they presented. Four categories were formed: (a) those with no symptoms, (b) those with one symptom only, (c) those with two or three symptoms and (d) those with four or more symptoms. It is true that sometimes one serious symptom can be more distressing than two mild symptoms, but since many psychological inventories use a numerical method of scoring we wanted to see what the number of symptoms might mean in terms of social functioning, consultation and psychiatric need. Of the total group, 12 per cent had one symptom only, 15 per cent had two or three and 10 per cent had more than three symptoms; women tended to have more symptoms than did men.

Sex differences and symptom groups

Analyses were carried out to see whether the men and women differed in the distribution of different symptom groups. As can be seen in Table 10.1, women have a higher prevalence of somatic symptoms compared with men. 30 per cent of women have one or more somatic symptoms (alone, or in conjunction with other 'psychological' symptoms) while only 17 per cent of the men fall into this category. On the other hand men have a higher proportion of respondents with psychological symptoms only. These differences are statistically significant at $p < \cdot 01$. Women were also found to have a significantly higher proportion than men of respondents with two or more symptoms.

A notable feature of the sex differences is that *psychotic* symptoms are much more common in men than in women. The numbers are too small for satisfactory statistical analysis, but the fact that the number of men who have psychotic symptoms is more than three times than that of women, although the total number of men in the sample is very much smaller than that of women, is very striking indeed.

Caste and symptom groups

Tables 10.3 and 10.4 show the distribution of the various symptom categories for males and females respectively.

TABLE 10.3

Symptom categories in the three caste groups
Males

	Brahmins (154)		Bants (55)		Mogers (217)	
	No.	%	No.	%	No.	%
1. Somatic sensory symptoms	20	13	10	18	25	12
2. Other somatic symptoms	10	15	8	15	24	11
3. Sleeplessness	14	9	8	15	28	13
4. Forgetfulness and poor concentration	16	10	2	4	22	10
5. Irritability and tension	7	5	3	6	9	4
6. Anxiety and worries	—	—	1	2	4	2
7. Depressive symptoms	8	5	—	—	9	4
8. Possession and hysterical fits	4	3	—	—	4	2
9. Psychotic symptoms	6	4	—	—	5	2
10. Epileptic fits	2	1	—	—	1	1
11. Mental retardation	3	2	—	—	—	—
12. Alcoholism	—	—	1	2	4	2

It can be seen that the Bants, both males and females, have a higher prevalence of most of the symptom groups than either Brahmins or Mogers. The difference is especially noticeable in the somatic categories and for sleeplessness. Bant males do not, however, have depressive or possession symptoms.

The highest possession rate is found amongst the Moger women.

The distribution in the psychosis category shows an interesting reversal of trend. While Brahmin males have a comparatively low prevalence of most of the symptom groups, they amongst the three caste groups have the highest proportion of those with psychotic symptoms. The numbers are too small for a statistical test of significance but the differences are nevertheless conspicuous.

An analysis was also carried out to examine the relative distribution of 'somatic' and 'psychological' symptoms in the three caste groups. The results once again confirmed the preponderance of somatic symptoms amongst the Bants, both men and women,

TABLE 10.4

Symptom cagegories in the three caste groups
Females

	Brahmins (299)		Bants (142)		Mogers (364)	
	No.	%	No.	%	No.	%
1. Somatic sensory symptoms	57	19	44	31	94	26
2. Other somatic symptoms	48	16	38	27	83	23
3. Sleeplessness	30	10	30	21	57	16
4. Forgetfulness and poor concentration	28	9	24	17	51	14
5. Tension and irritability	8	3	12	9	26	7
6. Anxiety and worries	2	1	3	2	2	1
7. Depressive symptoms	8	3	12	9	26	7
8. Possession and hysterical fits	4	1	1	1	21	6
9. Psychotic symptoms	3	1	1	1	1	1
10. Epileptic fits	1	1	1	1	2	1
11. Mental retardation	—	—	1	1	—	—
12. Alcoholism	—	—	—	—	—	—

although the differences were statistically significant only in case of women (p < ·05).

When the three caste groups were compared for the number of symptoms presented, significant differences were found only in the women; Brahmin women were less likely than women of the other two castes to have numerous symptoms.

Age and symptom groups

Analyses carried out according to the respondents' age distribution showed that the prevalence rates for epilepsy, psychosis, mental retardation and possession did not follow the general pattern of increase with age already demonstrated in the previous chapters. 50 per cent of the epileptics, psychotics and mentally retarded as a group were in the 15–20 age group, whereas only 10 per cent of all men and women with one or more symptoms were in this age category.

Possession was most commonly reported by people aged between 20–40; more than two-thirds of those suffering from possession state were in this age group while 37 per cent of all men and women with one or more symptoms belonged to this age category.

Education and symptom groups

It is commonly believed that psychiatric patients from 'primitive' cultures report somatic symptoms more commonly than the psychological symptoms. The explanation usually offered is that because of relatively poor language sophistication they find it easier to express their distress in 'body language' than in 'feeling language'. If this is true, the more educated people in these cultures should report fewer somatic symptoms than the less educated people. This hypothesis was put to the test by comparing the illiterate men and women in the Kota sample with those who had had some education, with respect to the relative distribution of 'somatic' and 'psychological' symptoms. (Those without any symptoms were excluded from this analysis.) The results were quite opposite to those expected. Among the literate people there was in fact a higher proportion of those with somatic symptoms. This was true for both men and women and the differences were statistically significant in both cases at $p < .01$.

Description of selected symptoms

Somatic symptons

The highest prevalence rates in the total Kota sample were found to be those of the two 'somatic' categories of symptoms. Most often, however, these occurred along with other, psychological symptoms; only 7 per cent of men and 12 per cent of women had somatic symptoms only.

It may well be questioned why these somatic symptoms are considered psychiatric at all. No one will deny that vague somatic complaints often have a psychological basis but it is very difficult to prove this beyond doubt, especially in a survey. A number of steps were taken in this study to ensure that there was sufficient circumstantial evidence in favour of those symptoms being of psychological origin.

Only those symptoms were inquired about which in the earlier pilot studies at the Bangalore mental hospital outpatient department were commonly reported by the psychiatric patients. A physical examination was carried out in every case with physical complaints, and anyone with even a suspicion of physical pathology was not included in this category. We realised that vague somatic symptoms are often the result of anaemia, malnutrition and helminthiasis, so common in poor countries. With this in view a study was carried out to examine the haemoglobin level and stools of 30 randomly selected members of each of the following four groups: those with no symptoms, those with somatic symptoms only, those with psychological symptoms only and those with both somatic and psychological symptoms.

The haemoglobin level was estimated by Sahli's method, and the stools were examined microscopically. It was found that there were no statistically significant differences in the mean haemoglobin levels nor in the proportions of those with amoebiasis or worms in the four groups. The mean haemoglobin levels were generally low, ranging from 9·9 to 10·2 grams per cent, while the proportion of those with amoebiasis or worms was more than 90 per cent in each category! This shows the poor health status of the Kota villagers but also proves that those who complained of 'somatic' symptoms did not have significantly more anaemia or infestation with worms than did the others.

Analyses were also carried out to see whether those factors which were found to be stressful and associated with higher 'case' rate (discussed in Chapter 9) were similarly related to the reporting of either somatic or psychological symptoms. It was found that higher age, poorer education status, poorer income status in males, widowhood in females and change-over to patrilineal system of residence were indeed positively correlated with both higher somatic symptom rates and higher psychological symptom rates. This indirectly suggests (since stress factors are similarly related to higher rates of both psychological and 'somatic' symptoms) that the latter may be of the same origin as the former.

On the basis of these findings we were as convinced as is possible in a survey of the psychological nature of the 'somatic' symptoms elicited in this study.

It may be interesting to consider some of these somatic symptoms in greater detail. 'Pains and aches' in various parts of the body formed the commonest symptom, followed closely by 'weakness'. Usually these two symptoms occurred together. It may be noted that these two symptoms were the commonest not only in the somatic categories but amongst all the symptoms elicited in the Kota sample.

A related system of beliefs concerns the concepts of bodily 'heat' and 'cold' which form an important element in the explanations of the causation of disease which one encounters in the Indian rural scene. In traditional Hindu culture, certain foods are regarded as 'hot' and others regarded as 'cold' in their effect. The actual temperature or taste of the food has nothing to do with its effect; in fact, the specific foods designated as hot or cold vary greatly from region to region within India. In Kota, for example, ice is considered a 'hot' food and pepper a 'cold' food, but these are local, not India-wide designations. Human beings must keep their 'heat' and 'cold' in balance, otherwise illness will occur. The centre of heat for men is in the head and that for women in the vagina. A man loses heat if there is excessive seminal discharge (semen is supposed to be derived from the brain heat) and a woman loses heat through childbirth.

Certain illnesses are supposed to be due to excessive heat, for example, headache, indigestion, skin diseases and violent mental illness. Others are supposed to be due to excessive cold, e.g. weakness, aches and pains, and depressive mental illness. When asked about the causes of their commonly reported weakness and aches and pains the women often ascribed this to the number of children they had had. Men were not as willing to admit excessive sexual indulgence in their own case, but the wise old men of the village were sure that this was an important cause of their troubles. Rice eating was given as another important cause; South Indians are a rice eating group and rice is a 'cold' food.

An interesting pointer to the relationship between cultural beliefs and symptom pattern can be seen in the distribution of headache as a symptom. While only 10 per cent of those with one or more somatic symptoms were in the below-20 age group, 50 per cent of the headache cases were in this category. Further, eight out of the twelve childless widows encountered in the sample complained of this symptom. Headache is supposed to be due to excessive 'heat', and younger people and childless widows are less likely to have lost their heat! The numbers are too small for statistical analysis but there is a sufficient indication that relationship between cultural beliefs as to the aetiology of symptoms and the perception of symptoms merits further exploration. It would be interesting, for example, to compare the symptomatology in the rice-eating South of India and in the wheat-eating North (wheat is a 'hot' food) using similar research techniques.

We found that education as such does not easily change these cultural beliefs. The educated people in Kota village talked of 'hot' and 'cold' food and of the supposed effects of sexual indulgence as much as and in fact more loquaciously than the illiterate villagers. Perhaps this is the reason why somatic symptoms were in fact found to be more common in the literate than in the illiterate people.

Possession states

Another area showing a close association between cultural beliefs and psychopathology was that of possession states.

We recorded as suffering from a possession state anyone who reported or was described as becoming possessed by a 'Bhuta' or 'Spirit' at least once during the preceding six months and who at such times behaved and spoke as though the possessing 'spirit' controlled his or her actions. People who had symptoms which they ascribed to spirits, but whose volition was not taken over by the spirit in the way described above, were not included in this category.

It is difficult to define this symptom as a delusion because in the study of attitudes mentioned earlier more than 60 per cent of the total sample believed that spirits exist and can affect individuals in this manner. Women believed in this more than men (men 32 per cent, women 80 per cent) and the percentage of women who shared this belief was highest (93 per cent) among Moger women.

Eight men and twenty-six women were found to have been possessed at least once in the last six months. While conducting the survey we discovered that there were two varieties of possession: those which are brought on voluntarily and those which visit the people against their will. We defined the two varieties as voluntary and involuntary possessions.

The distribution of the voluntary and involuntary possessions in the different caste and sex groups is given in Table 10.5.

TABLE 10.5

Voluntary and involuntary possession states

		Brahmins	Bants	Mogers	Total
Males:	Voluntary	4	—	2	6
	Involuntary	—	—	2	2
Females:	Voluntary	—	—	16	16
	Involuntary	4	1	5	10

In general those with voluntary possessions were not disturbed by these occurrences and were revered by those around them as being endowed with special powers. At times of illness or distress in the family or neighbourhood these individuals would summon their spirit, become possessed and offer some solution to the problem. All the four Brahmin men, two of the Moger men and two of the sixteen Moger women with voluntary possessions were actually earning their living in this way, as Darshana-Patris. It was obvious that the other two Moger men and fourteen Moger women in this group were certainly gaining a great deal in terms of status if not in money through their affliction.

There were two involuntary possessions amongst men, but ten women suffered from this condition. Suffering is the correct word because unlike those with voluntary possessions, these women were not happy with their affliction and in fact resented it.

The pattern of possessions was very similar in all cases, voluntary or involuntary. The description of one particular case which was observed will serve to illustrate the phenomenon: this was a 30-year-old woman, an agricultural labourer who became possessed after being abused by her sister-in-law during a quarrel. She started by making monotonous, mumbling sounds in her mouth and white froth appeared on her lips. Following this her body started shivering and she fell down. She kicked her legs around on the ground and announced that she was the spirit of her husband's dead grandmother. The spirit shouted in high emotion that she had now come to stay in the house and would only leave after causing destruction. A dialogue then followed between the spirit and the relatives who had collected around her, in the course of which it became apparent that the dead person's spirit had not been sufficiently propitiated. A special ceremony was promised and the spirit went away. The woman became unconscious and woke up after five minutes not knowing what had happened.

It is commonly believed that possession state is a hysterical phenomenon—a symbolic representation of some deep unconscious conflict. Undoubtedly the pattern of the fit seems bizarre to an alien onlooker. We find it difficult to believe, however, that voluntary possessions are hysterical phenomena. It seems to us that, in a culture in which a belief in Bhutas and Spirits is common, this is one of the acceptable ways of earning status in the society and often of making a living. The involuntary possessions are in all likelihood distress signals; in each of the ten cases there was evidence of family disharmony. Our study was not, however, designed to make a systematic investigation of family interactions.

Psychosis

Eleven men and five women had one or more psychotic symptoms, by which we mean delusions, hallucinations, unintelligible speech, bizarre behaviour or disorientation of a nature or intensity which proved culturally unacceptable to their fellows. One man and two women had psychotic symptoms together with epilepsy. Two men had advanced neurological symptoms and were diagnosed as suffering from organic psychosis of old age. There were, therefore, seven men and three women who had neither epilepsy nor organic damage and could safely be regarded as suffering from functional psychosis.

One man out of these seven suffered from persecutory delusions only; the other nine men and women appeared to be showing features of chronic schizophrenia. There was no one who could be diagnosed as manic-depressive, though a history of what sounded like chronic mania was given concerning one man.

The distribution of psychosis by sex and caste was very peculiar. Males outnumbered females by seven to three, although women outnumbered men in the total sample by nearly two to one. Even more peculiar was the fact that while the Brahmin males showed the lowest 'case' rate, no fewer than six out of the seven male functional psychotics were Brahmins! These numbers are too small for a satisfactory statistical analysis but there is no doubt that the male Brahmins showed a psychosis rate much higher than could be expected. This excess was not associated with an excess of consanguineous marriages, which occurred with similar frequency in the three castes.

Schizophrenic psychosis is generally believed to be an illness of bio-chemical origin and is not expected to differ in prevalence in the different cultural groups. A contrary view has been advanced at various times to the effect that schizophrenia is an illness of the more sophisticated cultures, and Torrey (1973) has recently assembled evidence in favour of this view. There is no doubt that the Brahmins of Kota represent a more sophisticated culture than that of the Bants and Mogers*, hence Torrey's claim seems to be supported by our findings. This could, of course, be a purely chance finding and we wait for another study comparing these groups to confirm or disprove what we discovered.

Depressive symptoms

Our study provides one more proof that depressive symptoms are not limited to western societies. In fact the numbers of those with depressive symptoms in our study were quite substantial—17 men and 21 women. Proportionately men suffered from depressive symptoms more often than women. Loss of interest, suicidal feelings, and feelings of incompetence were very common in this group. (In a separate inquiry fifteen people were reported to have committed suicide and four known to have attempted suicide in the whole village during the past three years.) None of the Bant men in the sample had depressive symptoms. This may be due to the small size of the sample of Bant men rather than to any special attribute of this caste group since the Bant women have a high rate (9 per cent) for reporting such symptoms.

---

* This is not meant in any derogatory sense—only in the sense of academic and technical achievement and attitudes towards modernisation.

Infrequent symptoms

No respondent described obsessive-compulsive symptoms. Only four men expressed worries about loss of semen in the urine or about masturbation (three Brahmins and one Moger). It is difficult to believe that these figures represent the true state of affairs; clinical experience elsewhere in India (Carstairs, 1956) leads us to believe that symptoms of this kind are widespread but not readily admitted. Only five men, all Mogers, were found to be suffering from excessive drinking beyond their cultural norm. In all the five there was evidence of malnutrition and all of them were claimed to be 'parasites' by their family members.

Summary

1. Women have higher prevalence of somatic symptoms than men. They also have a higher proportion of those with numerous symptoms.

2. Bants have more somatic symptoms than Brahmins or Mogers. Moger women have the highest possession rate. Brahmin males have the highest proportion of those with psychotic symptoms.

3. Psychosis, epilepsy and mental retardation are commonest in those below 20. Possession occurs most often in those between 20 and 40 years of age.

4. Somatic symptoms appear to be more commonly reported by literates as compared to illiterates. The nature of somatic symptoms reflects prevailing cultural beliefs.

CONSULTATION, ABILITY TO COPE
AND SOCIAL FUNCTIONING

To whom does one turn to in pain, sickness or distress? We have explored this question already and have also described the results of an attitude study designed to investigate which of the local healers were likely to be consulted first for a given check list of symptoms. We continued to pursue this line of investigation, and in the survey of mental disorder everyone with one or more symptoms was asked this additional question: 'Have you consulted anyone for this trouble?' Those who answered in the affirmative were asked to name the agency or agencies they had visited. Whenever a relative was also given a detailed IPSS interview, he or she was asked to supplement the information given by the subject himself. No attempt was made to inquire who was first consulted or how many times, since during our pilot studies we had discovered that the respondents were hazy about the exact order and number of times various healers had been visited.

The information was recorded in seven precoded categories, consultation noted as having been made with a (1) Doctor—trained in Western medicine; (2) Vaid—trained in Indian medicine; (3) Mantarwadi—making use of potent holy verses and astrology; (4) Patri—the medium acting with the authority of the spirit which possessed him; (5) the Temple Priest; (6) Family Elder; and (7) any other helper.

The Family Elder was kept as a separate category because frequently the older members of the household know of and dispense remedies passed on to them by their ancestors. The category 'any other helper' referred to consultations which could not be accommodated under the other headings, for example, those made with a visiting Swami or with agencies advertised in the newspapers.

The information obtained from the subject and that from his relative (when interviewed) were combined during the analysis. For example, if the subject reported having seen a doctor, and the relative reported that a Mantarwadi had been contacted, consultation was recorded as having been made both with a Doctor and a Mantarwadi.

In the description which follows, the terms 'consultation' and 'consulters' refer to any contact with a healer *since the onset of the present symptoms*, the point of onset being determined by the respondent. Where a contact with a doctor is contrasted with that with other agencies as a group, the former is called an 'allopathic' consultation and the latter an 'indigenous' consultation. The term 'symptom group' refers to all those respondents who had one or more symptoms.

Sex differences in consultation

59 per cent of men and precisely the same percentage of women belonging to the symptom group had consulted one or more agencies since the onset of symptoms. There are, therefore, no sex differences in the proportion of consulters.

Those who had made one or more consultation were further divided into three groups: those who had made allopathic consultation only, those who had consulted both an allopathic and an indigenous practitioner and those who had consulted an indigenous practitioner only.

TABLE 11.1

Type of consultation

Type of consultation	Males (80) %	Females (188) %	Total (268) %
Allopathic only	30	44	40
Allopathic and indigenous	48	48	46
Indigenous only	23	10	14.

The table shows that the consultation rate is highest with a western-trained doctor and that the women consult a doctor more often than do the men.

Among the women there was a higher proportion of those who made an allopathic consultation only, while the men showed a higher proportion of those who made an indigenous consultation only. The differences were found on chi-square test to be statistically significant at $p < \cdot 05$. This was surprising; men being more educated and more 'modern' should have been expected to lean towards a western-trained doctor more heavily than women. Our findings are, however, consistent with those in the attitude study described earlier (Chapter 5) where, compared with men, the women showed a greater preference for a doctor as the first source of help in case of illness.

We discussed this odd finding with informants in the village and discovered that the women were apprehensive of going to Mantar-wadis and Patris because of the excessive 'sexual heat' these people are believed to be endowed with, giving them power to attract women. This also explained the reason why in the clinics of the indigenous healers men outnumbered the women to such a great extent, and why, even when the healer was consulted about a woman's trouble, it was often a man of the family who took the complaints to these healers. No such situation was observed in the clinics of the doctors where women were seen as often as the men.

Type of symptoms

Consultation rates were compared in those with somatic symptoms only, those with psychological symptoms only and those with both somatic and psychological symptoms.

We found that those with 'psychological symptoms only' showed the lowest proportion of consulters. Men of this group have, however, a higher proportion of consulters (48 per cent) than women (27 per cent). A further analysis was carried out to see whether the type of consultation also differed in people with different types of symptoms. In general, patients with 'psychological symptoms only' were less likely to consult any type of healer. We found that respondents with 'somatic symptoms only' were more likely to consult a doctor than an indigenous healer, whereas the reverse was true of those reporting 'psychological symptoms only'. It will not surprise anyone familiar with Indian village life to learn that there was a strong tendency to consult both types of healer, whatever the complaint.

Next, an analysis was carried out to see whether those who had symptoms in the different hierarchical categories differed in consultation rates. Because of small numbers, men and women were combined in this analysis. It was found that the consultation rate was 100 per cent for both the epileptics and psychotics. However, while all the epileptics had seen a doctor trained in Western medicine, only six out of thirteen psychotics had done so; the others having gone only to a Mantarwadi or a Patri.

The consultation rate was 42 per cent in the combined 'de-pression' and 'anxiety' categories, 51 per cent in the 'other neurotic' category and 67 per cent in the 'somatic' category. Those with Possession had the lowest proportion of consulters—26 per cent. We carried out further analyses to see whether those who reported voluntary possession consulted helping agencies—for any psychiatric symptoms revealed in our survey, and not necessarily on account of their possession—with the same frequency as those with involuntary possession. It was found that six out of ten women with involuntary possession had consulted, while only three out of the sixteen women with voluntary possession had consulted. This further supports our thesis that voluntary possession in the absence of other symptoms is unlikely to be an indicator of mental distress.

Number of symptoms

Table 11.2 shows the difference in consultation rate amongst those with different numbers of symptoms.

TABLE 11.2

Number of symptoms and consultation

		1 symptom only	2–3 symptoms	4 or more symptoms
Males:	Total	57	47	31
	Percentage of consulters	39%	68%	77%
Females:	Total	94	121	105
	Percentage of consulters	36%	64%	68%

It can be seen that the higher the number of symptoms, the higher is the proportion of consulters. This is true for both men and women.

Socio-demographic correlates of consultation

An analysis was carried out to see whether those in the different age, education, income, family type and marital status groups differed in the proportion of consulters. No statistically significant differences were seen. Another analysis was carried out to see whether the different groups differed in the type of consultation (allopathic vs indigenous). Once again no statistically significant differences were seen, nor was any consistent trend observed.

The lack of relationship between age, education and income on the one hand and consultation on the other is an interesting negative finding. We had expected that the more educated, because of their modern views, and the young, because they include a higher proportion of the educated, would patronise a doctor more often. We had also expected that the rich would make a greater use of the more expensive doctor as compared with the poor. These expectations were not fulfilled.

The conclusion we draw is that the real attitudes in relation to consultation, which as it happens are becoming more favourable to doctors, are not influenced by expressed 'modernity' nor by school education. From our discussions with the villagers we discovered that doctors were being preferred not because the indigenous healers were considered to be working from wrong concepts, but because of the former's ability to show better results. For the same reason the poor did not hesitate to go to a slightly more expensive doctor when he was considered to be the right person for the job.

When we compared the proportions of members of the three castes who consulted any agency—considering only those with one or more symptoms in this analysis—we found that Bants (both men and women) had a higher proportion of consulters than either the Brahmins or the Mogers. Members of the three caste groups did not, however, show any consistent bias in preference for consulting either allopathic or indigenous healers.

Summary and comments

1. The most favoured agency of consultation is a western-trained doctor. This is consistent with the attitudes towards consultation described in Chapter 5.

2. People with psychological symptoms only have a much lower consultation rate than those with somatic symptoms only or those with both somatic and psychological symptoms. It seems that to suffer from a psychological symptom provides a less acceptable pretext for consultations, especially with a western-trained doctor.

3. Both epilepsy and psychosis are considered serious enough by the villagers to require consultation in 100 per cent of cases. It is interesting, however, to see that out of the thirteen in the psychosis group only six had been to a Western doctor. None of the thirteen had seen a Western doctor only. For psychosis, Western medicine does not seem to be the agency of first choice.

4. The lowest consultation rate is for possession. This, together with the still lower rates for voluntary possession, supports our contention that possession is in many cases only a socially approved method of acquiring status or earning money and not a symptom of disorder.

5. There are no sex differences in the proportion of consulters but the women show a relatively higher preference for consulting a western-trained doctor, rather than an indigenous agency, as compared with the men.

6. The Bants (both men and women) have, compared with the other caste groups, a higher proportion of consulters. If consultation is any indication of the seriousness a person ascribes to his or her symptoms, Bants have not only a higher 'case' rate (as shown in

Chapter 10) but also a higher rate for symptoms perceived as serious.

7. The reporting of more than one symptom appears to be a very good indicator of the likelihood of consultation; the greater the number of symptoms, the greater is the proportion of consulters.

Inability to cope

Consultation is only one way of revealing that the symptoms are distressful. There are people who are distressed and who feel that their symptoms interfere with a full life but who for one reason or another do not make a consultation. To elicit the proportion of such people in the sample, a question was asked of everyone with one or more symptoms: 'Do you feel that because of your symptoms you are unable to cope with your work and social relations?' The answers were recorded in simple 'Yes' and 'No' categories. For the sake of simplicity those who expressed difficulty, but not a complete inability to cope were also included in the 'unable to cope' group. Those who were sure that their symptoms did not affect their work and social relations were labelled as 'able to cope'.

53 per cent of men and 56 per cent of women with one or more symptoms declared an inability to cope. There are therefore no sex differences in this dimension.

Those with somatic symptoms only were compared with those with psychological symptoms. No statistically significant differences in ability to cope were noticed. An analysis was carried out to examine the relationship between number of symptoms and inability to cope. The results are shown in Table 11.3.

TABLE 11.3

Number of symptoms and being 'unable to cope'

	1 symptom only	2–3 symptoms	4 + symptoms
	%	%	%
Percentage of males who were 'unable to cope'	35	66	68
Percentage of females who were 'unable to cope'	40	53	76

It can be seen that the greater the number of symptoms, the higher is the proportion of those with declared inability to cope.

When a further analysis was carried out to examine coping ability in relation to the different hierarchical categories of symptoms, it was found that only 57 per cent of the epileptics declared that they were unable to cope, although all of them have consulted. A majority of the psychotics were unable to co-operate in this inquiry because of their symptoms, and this in itself was taken as evidence of their inability to cope; nevertheless four out of the thirteen who reported psychotic symptoms declared themselves able to cope.

60 per cent of the combined depression and anxiety group declared inability to cope, as compared with 56 per cent of the 'other neurotics' and 51 per cent of the somatic group. Only 30 per cent of the possession group declared this inability.

When respondents with symptoms of depression or anxiety were compared with those who complained only of 'somatic' symptoms, the former group contained more members who declared themselves 'unable to cope', and fewer who consulted any healer, whereas the reverse was true for the latter group. It seems, therefore, that in this Indian village, just as in the Western world, patients find it easier to consult about physical than about emotional symptoms of distress.

Caste and ability to cope

The proportion of those unable to cope was compared in members of the three caste groups who reported symptoms of any kind. It was found that the Bants had the highest proportion of those unable to cope and the Brahmins the lowest. The difference was most marked for the males, among whom 81 per cent of the Bants, but only 48 per cent of the Brahmins or the Mogers who had symptoms reported themselves as unable to cope. Among the women, the Brahmins (33 per cent disabled) differed markedly from both the Mogers (66 per cent) and the Bants (70 per cent disabled).

Analyses were carried out to examine the relationship of age, education, income, family type and marital status to coping ability. No statistically significant relationships were observed.

To summarise

1. There are no sex differences in the proportions of respondents with symptoms who declared themselves unable to cope.

2. Bants have not only the highest 'case' rate and the highest proportion of consulters but also the highest proportion of those with symptoms who declared themselves unable to cope.

3. 'Inability to cope' has no demonstrable correlation with other socio-demographic factors such as age, education, income, family type and marital status.

4. The greater the number of symptoms, the greater is the declared inability to cope.

5. The depressive and the anxious have a higher proportion of

those unable to cope than those in the somatic group but the proportion of consulters is quite the opposite in the two groups. This supports the inference made earlier that somatic symptoms are more acceptable as the occasion for consulting a healer than are purely psychological symptoms.

Symptoms and social functioning

Those with and without symptoms were compared for their scores in different aspects of social functioning. The comparisons were made separately for the different caste, age and sex categories. This was necessary because in our sample those with and without symptoms were unequally balanced for caste, age and sex ratios, and we had already discovered that these variables influenced the social functioning scores. Scores for 'work', 'entertainments', 'visits' and 'religious participation' were tackled separately. Sexual functioning (declared frequency of sexual intercourse) was examined only for married men below 50. 'Time spent with children in the evening' was examined only in men who had one or more children of their own. Student's 't' test after log transformation of the scores (because of the latter's skewness) was applied to compare the means.

Only in the case of Brahmin men below the age of 20 did we find that those with one or more symptoms had significantly lower work, religious participation and entertainment scores compared with those without symptoms. In all other comparisons, though those with symptoms often showed decidedly lower mean scores, no statistical significant difference was observed. In our opinion the lack of statistical significance is due to the fact that, in our attempts to make the questionnaire meet the strict methodological requirements outlined in Chapter 7, we omitted precisely those questions which might have been able to tap the subtle aspects of functioning which are affected by presence of symptoms. We ascribe the lower scores of young Brahmin men, with symptoms, to the inclusion in this group of several psychotics who failed to meet even the minimal expectations tested by this questionnaire.

Since in general the scores did not distinguish between those with and without symptoms, social functioning as measured by this questionnaire was not included in the measure of need, for obvious reasons. Our hope that we could develop a measure of social functioning which would be quite independent of observations of psychological symptoms, was disappointed. Perhaps this is in fact an unrealisable aim; but, before abandoning it altogether, we hope that further attempts will be made—by other workers, if not by ourselves—to find ways of objectively recording degrees of impair-

ment of performance of customary social roles, using parameters
uncontaminated by indicators of psychiatric disorder.

Social stress and mental disorder

While reviewing the differences between the matrilineal and the
patrilineal caste groups in our study we soon became aware of the
other ways in which some members of particular castes were being
exposed to new forms of stress. For example, the Mogers who till
recently were ritually, socially and economically inferior to the
Bants were now suddenly becoming richer, and this distressed the
Bants. On the one hand there was the traditional competition with
those Brahmins who were farmers like themselves, and on the other
hand there was this growing threat to their social status from the
Mogers! At one time there was a hope that the Indian Land Act,
which was designed to give the land to the tiller, would benefit the
Bants who are mainly tenant farmers; but, as numerous social
commentators have pointed out, there was a long enough delay in
the application of the law to allow the land-owning Brahmins to
reorganise themselves in such a fashion that the land did not slip
out of their hands. This has created a sense of hoplessness amongst
the Bants. They also complain that, in spite of their being nearly as
well educated as the Brahmins, the best jobs go to the latter. As
mentioned earlier, employment in government and other service
jobs is obtained by Brahmins to a degree out of proportion to their
numbers in the community.

It is not surprising, therefore, that Bants were found to have the
highest frequency of mental disorder. To recapitulate:

1. 39 per cent of the male Bants had one or more symptoms
compared with 32 per cent of Mogers and 29 per cent of Brahmins.

2. 81 per cent of the male Bants with one or more symptoms
consulted someone for relief as compared with 52 per cent each of
Brahmins and Mogers.

3. 81 per cent of the male Bants with symptoms declared an
inability to cope as compared with only 48 per cent each of
Brahmins and Mogers.

4. 15 per cent of the male Bants were rated as showing moderately
high to very high need for some form of attention or support as
compared with 11 per cent of the Brahmins and 12 per cent of the
Mogers.

Among females the story is slightly different. The changes in the
conjugal residence pattern, which for obvious reasons influence
females much more than men, appear to be a greater source of stress
than the insecurity of social and economic status which influences

the men more. As a result Bant and Moger women, influenced as both are by changes in residence, present equal rates of mental disorder which are both significantly higher than the rate shown by Brahmin women. To recapitulate:

1. 43 per cent of the Bant and 42 per cent of the Moger females have one or more symptoms compared with 33 per cent of the Brahmins.

2. 70 per cent of the Bant and 66 per cent of the Moger females with symptoms declared an inability to cope compared with only 33 per cent of the Brahmins.

3. 22 per cent of the Bant and 21 per cent of the Moger females had moderately high to high need for help as compared with only 9 per cent of the Brahmins.

It might appear that we are being too simplistic in putting the entire blame for higher mental disorder in Bant and Moger females to their being distressed by insecure living conditions. We only claim that the shift in residence is *one* of the most important factors, and the claim would not appear exaggerated if we remember that the rate of those with symptoms among Bant and Moger women who had not changed their residence pattern was 36 per cent, only 3 per cent higher than that of Brahmin women, while the corresponding rate was 53 per cent in case of those who had changed!

Another factor which might have been expected to influence the mental disorder rate was that of family constitution. No differences were found between those living in joint family and in nuclear family settings respectively. Perhaps the advantages and disadvantages of the two kinds of family setting are equally balanced.

It might be argued that the postulated stress factors on which we have commented are too general and superficial, while there are many other causes of stress which are peculiar to specific situations and which were not examined in this study. This is true, but a depth study of stress factors is not compatible with the epidemiological approach adopted in this inquiry.

We have found that the Bants of Kota have a higher mental disorder rate than Brahmins and Mogers. This does not necessarily mean that as a group Bants are more prone to mental disorder; an equally plausible explanation is that in this particular area they are experiencing greater stress. Another group of Bants, living not far away in the southern part of South Kanara, are known to live in much happier circumstances and in fact are reported to be the most influential group in the area. It seems highly likely that Bants living under those conditions may show quite different rates for emotionally determined symptoms.

12

MEASUREMENT OF NEED

In our survey, 32 per cent of men and 40 per cent of women were found to have one or more symptoms. Not all of them could be assumed to be in need of help and treatment, at least not to the same extent. In Chapter 1 we have discussed at length the complexities involved in assessing the degree of need but, difficult as the question is to answer, it must be tackled if the 'case' rates determined by an epidemiologist are to have some meaning for the health planners, whose job it is to allocate priorities in utilisation of resources. The planners must be told what proportion of the population have psychiatric problems needing urgent attention, what proportion can wait a little longer, and what proportion do not need any help at all.

We have already mentioned that some attempt was made in the Stirling County study and in the Midtown Manhattan study to estimate the priorities for attention, but the criteria used were partly subjective and reflected the value judgements of the investigators rather than those of the populations being assessed. In the Kota study we planned to make a combined use of four different criteria, namely:

(a) Presence, and number, of psychiatric symptoms
(b) Consultation for relief of these symptoms
(c) Inability to cope because of symptoms, and
(d) Social dysfunctioning as a result of symptoms.

These criteria represent only a few of the possible determinants of need but had the advantage of being simple, explicit and free from the value judgements of the investigators. Unfortunately, as we progressed with the study we came face-to-face with unsurmountable problems inherent in the measurement of social functioning and decided to forego that as a criterion.

It is obvious that a person who has consulted someone for relief of symptoms has already indicated his desire for help. Much has been written about the 'sick role' and the influence of personality as well as of socio-demographic factors in determining it (Mechanic, 1972). It is true that people with certain characteristics are more likely to choose a 'sick role' and consult, compared with others who show the same pathology. It is not difficult, however, to accept that these people may experience a less intense degree of subjective distress;

and since, in the field of psychiatry, subjective distress enters into the very definitions of symptoms, one is persuaded to accept consultation as an indisputable signal of need.

It may be added that in rural India a consultation reflects the felt need not only of the individual but of the whole family. In a typical household an individual may express his distress or be noted by those around him to be disturbed, but the decision about taking him to a healer, and to which healer, is taken by the family. Hardly ever does the individual visit a healer without an accompanying family member, and quite often the relatives go to consult a healer without taking the 'patient' with them!

This is not true of declared 'inability to cope', which is a personal feeling and with which the other family members may or may not agree. However, the fact that a family did not opt for consultation does not necessarily mean that one of its members is not in need of help. What are we trying to stress is that though to a large extent consultation and inability to cope cover the same ground they also severally tap different aspects of need, the former that of the family and the latter that of the individual. That they represent something similar is shown by the fact that the two were positively correlated (showing a tetrachoric correlation coefficient of $+ \cdot 43$). That they measure something different also is shown by the fact that the 'depressives' and 'anxious' had a higher proportion of those unable to cope and a lower proportion of consulters, while the opposite was true for people in the 'somatic' group.

It was decided to combine these two measures of need into a common 'distress scale'. Anyone who had neither consulted nor expressed an inability to cope was given a score of '0'; anyone who either consulted *or* declared an inability to cope was given a score of '1', and anyone who consulted as well as declared an inability to cope was given a score of '2'.

We also decided to derive a more differentiated criterion from the observed 'presence of symptoms'. It had already been discovered that the number of symptoms bore a close relation to both consultation and inability to cope; the greater the number of symptoms the higher were the proportions of consulters and of those unable to cope. The number of symptoms was therefore closely related to distress and was accepted as another measure of need.

Those with no symptoms at all were given a score of '0'. Those with one symptom only were given a score of '1', those with two or three symptoms were given a score of '2', and those with four or more symptoms were given a score of '3'. This was called the 'symptom scale'.

The Symptom scale and the Distress scale were found to have a positive correlation of +·34 (Kendall's rank order correlation) and were combined into a common 'Need scale' by adding together the unweighted scores on each of these two csales.

On the Need scale a person could score from 'o' to '5'. 'o' for one who had no symptoms at all and '5' for one who had four or more symptoms, had consulted and had declared an inability to cope.

Table 12.1 shows the distribution of respondents on the 'Need scale'.

TABLE 12.1

Distribution of the total sample on the need scale

Need score	Population (1233)	
	No.	%
0	778	63
1	70	6
2	81	7
3	117	9
4	112	9
5	75	6

It can be seen that 6 per cent of the total population score '5', i.e. have the highest need for help and treatment. At the other end of the scale, another 6 per cent of the population score '1', that is, have one symptom only and have neither consulted nor expressed an inability to cope. In any allocation of priorities the 6 per cent who score '5' will be accorded the highest priority for attention, and the 6 per cent who score '1' will be judged to have a very low priority.

What proof is there that those with the highest scores really have the greatest need for help? There is in fact none except that provided through common sense. These people have the highest number of symptoms which make them unable to cope with work and social relations and which force them to consult someone. In the absence of a valid, absolute external criterion for need only circumstantial evidence can be provided. The fact that the distress and symptom scales have high positive correlation shows that the items chosen for the Need scale have at least got concurrent validity.

Evidence in support of the validity of the Need scale was provided when it was discovered that ten out of the thirteen respondents with psychotic symptoms had scored '5', while the other three had scored '4' on this scale. There can be little doubt that psychotics have in general the greatest need for help and treatment, and when the

Need scale tells the same story it confirms the meaningfulness of the latter.

It may be argued that one does not require to use a Need scale in order to identify psychotics, but the advantage of the scale is that it points out those who score the same as the psychotics and who, therefore, out of all those with psychiatric symptoms, require attention no less urgently.

What cut-off point should be used when trying to estimate psychiatric case rates? Once again there can be no automatic choice for the cut-off point; it depends on the resources available. If resources are meagre one could limit one's attention to the top 6 per cent, but if the resources are more plentiful, one may include all those scoring '4' on the Need scale; this would give a case rate of 15 per cent. This rate would incidentally include all the psychotics, all the epileptics, 68 per cent of the depressives, 54 per cent of the anxious, 42 per cent of the other neurotics, 50 per cent of those with possession and 23 per cent of those with somatic symptoms. These rates are worked out from our hierarchical classification of symptoms. One more proof of the validity of the Need scale is that this case rate of 15 per cent would include ten out of twelve respondents with involuntary possession but only five out of the twenty-two with voluntary possession. We have repeatedly stated that voluntary possession is rarely a psychiatric symptom. We based our conclusion on other evidence, but the Need scale scores are consonant with our views.

Caste and psychiatric need

An analysis was carried out to compare the need-based case rates amongst the three caste groups. Table 12.2 shows the comparison when the case rate was taken as 15 per cent, i.e. considering only those as cases who scored '4' or '5' on the Need scale.

TABLE 12.2

Caste and need-based case rates
(Using scores of 4 or 5 on the Need scale as criterion)

		Brahmins	Bants	Mogers	Total
Males:	Total	154	55	217	426
	Case rate	11%	15%	12%	12%
Females:	Total	299	143	365	807
	Case rate	9%	22%	21%	17%

It can be seen that among the males Bants have a slightly higher case rates than Brahmins or Bants, and among the females Bants and

Mogers both have a much higher case rate than the Brahmins. Women as a group have higher case rates than men.

It is interesting to note that the caste and sex differences in the Need-based rates are in the same direction and roughly of same proportion as when a case was defined as anyone with one or more symptoms.

To summarise

1. A Need scale was formed by combining the criteria of consultation, inability to cope and number of symptoms, each of the variables being positively correlated with each other.

2. The validity of the Need scale was supported when the psychotics, who would generally be considered as having higher need, also scored high on this scale and when cases with voluntary possession, who from other evidence were considered by us not necessarily to be regarded as psychiatric cases at all, scored low on the Need scale.

3. 6 per cent of the population fell into the highest need category, but the cut-off point (4 or above) which picked out all the psychotics and epileptics gave a figure of 15 per cent as the case rate in the total population.

4. Considering only those scoring 4 or more as 'cases', Bant and Moger women were found to have the highest case rates. Women as a group had a higher case rate than men.

13

MEETING THE NEEDS IN A DEVELOPING COUNTRY

The pilot survey of psychiatric symptoms, carried out in the village of Sakalwada during the preparatory stage of this inquiry, surprised us by revealing a high prevalence of such symptoms in a rather typical rural community. Subsequently, this was confirmed in the major survey. Perhaps we should not have been surprised. The history of psychiatry has been punctuated with the discovery—and rediscovery—of this simple fact, that minor degrees of mental ill-health, manifesting as depression, neuroses or psychosomatic disorders, are very widespread indeed. Already in 1689 Thomas Sydenham encountered such conditions in one-sixth of all his patients, while in 1733 another London physician, George Cheyne, reported a still higher frequency of emotionally-determined symptoms in his clientele; in his book *The English Disease* he described 'hysteria' as the commonest condition in his practice.

Throughout the 18th century medical writers, particularly in the German literature, were much interested in the physical accompaniments of disturbances of the emotions; but then, and for many years to come, vulnerability to such ailments was regarded as an attribute of highly cultivated, intellectually advanced and correspondingly hypersensitive indivuduals. Members of the 'lower orders' of society, and so-called 'primitive peoples' were believed to be relatively immune from emotional disorders. Undoubtedly, they were unable to find words with which to describe their feelings, and in many cases they were so fully engaged in the struggle for survival that they had little time for introspection; Sydenham noticed that hysterical symptoms were commoner in women who employed servants than in those who had to work with their hands. Nevertheless, even the most inarticulate persons can experience grief, disappointment, frustration, fear and anger—and may do so all the more intensely because of their inability to express their feelings verbally.

In the West, recent morbidity surveys have again revealed the high rate of prevalence of emotional disorders, not least among the poorest sections of the population, who are aware only of symptoms of physical distress, for which they seek relief from a bottle of medicine, from a tranquilliser or from recourse to alcohol. Psychiatrists have been disconcerted to find that they and these lower-class patients 'do not talk the same language' where these disorders are concerned, and hence find great difficulty in establishing a fruitful therapeutic relationship.

A similar deadlock can be observed in many of the developing countries. Here, too, numerous morbidity surveys have shown high rates of prevalence of psychiatric symptoms, severe enough to cause distress and to prompt many people to consult traditional healers, in the hope of obtaining relief. One of the most striking demonstrations of this was reported a few years ago by Giel and Van Luijk (1969), two Dutch epidemiologists working in Ethiopia. They screened the population of a small town in that country and found that five per cent of its semi-rural population had some psychiatric symptoms, with at least a mild degree of impairment of function, at the time of their survey. Shortly after this, they examined a representative sample of all outpatients attending the major General Hospital in Addis Ababa and found that over 18 per cent of these patients were suffering primarily from psychiatric rather than physical disorders. Similar findings have been reported from general hospitals in Africa, India, Indonesia, Pakistan, Egypt and Tunisia— indeed from every country where psychiatrically trained investigators have taken the trouble to carry our such a survey.

For many years, health planners in the developing countries have (quite properly) devoted their attention to combatting the killing diseases, particularly those due to infection by bacteria or parasites. It is well known that the best way to control these diseases is to improve standards of sanitation, and to provide safe drinking water. Sometimes, in addition, steps can be taken to break the chain of infection: for example, massive campaigns of DDT spraying of village houses can almost wipe out the mosquito whose bite transmits malaria, and thus eradicate that disease from regions where it has long been endemic; and the inoculation of whole populations against smallpox can similarly arrest its spread, and eventually cause its disappearance.

The most striking advances in public health have been made through preventive programmes of this kind. There have also been a few demonstrations of the successful eradication of long-established disease by a potent remedy—for example the painful tropical skin disease called yaws has yielded to single massive doses of penicillin; and in some Western countries tuberculosis has been all but wiped out by new and potent medicines, which are still, unfortunately, too costly and too slow-acting to be readily acceptable in the poor countries of the world.

Already, during the quarter-century following the Second World War, we have seen great changes in the pattern of morbidity in the West. The major forms of morbidity are no longer the infections, but the chronic and disabling conditions—and the neuroses. This is bringing about a major change in the very concept of disease. Hitherto, it has been possible to think of disease as an invasion of the 'naturally' healthy person by malign influences from the outer environment. In traditional societies, these were (and still are) believed to be supernatural forces, the manifestations of gods, demons, witches or sorcerers, while in technologically advanced societies particularly toxins and infections came to be identified as the cause of ill-health; but today, more than ever before, the human species is being revealed as its own worst enemy. Some of the commonest killers in the West, such as road accidents, heart disease, and suicide are now recognised as being attributable to pathological patterns of behaviour on the part of individuals, and of groups. This is even more obvious in the case of attempted suicide—which today accounts for 10 per cent of all admissions to acute medical services in most Western countries—and of neuroses and psychosomatic disorders, in which the underlying pathology is to be found in pathological interpersonal relationships.

The implications of this realisation are so enormous that most people have simply avoided facing them. Not only the planners of health services, but also those responsible for social welfare seemed to be unnerved by the thought that every year one person in ten in the entire population may need help in dealing with emotionally-determined symptoms. One reaction is simply to dismiss such symptoms as unimportant. After all, neurosis does not kill, so it can be safely ignored, and health services can continue to concentrate on displaying the wonders of scientific medicine in modern hospitals and private clinics, while the social services are already fully engaged in dealing with the social pathology which seems to be an inevitable accompaniment of industrialisation and urbanisation— problems of poverty, broken homes, child neglect, delinquency, alcoholism and crime.

However, there are at least three important groups of people who have not been content to dismiss symptoms of anxiety, or of psychosomatic illness, as unimportant. First, there are the manufacturers of so-called 'psychotropic' drugs, the tranquillisers and the mood-elevators. During the last twenty years vast fortunes have been made by the sales of these drugs, and even today very large sums of money are spent on competitive advertising, designed to convince doctors—and patients—that for every form of emotional distress there is a patent remedy. In the West, a generation of doctors whose medical training included very little instruction in psychopathology has tended, on the whole, to rely on these drugs which offer their patients temporary relief, even though the problems underlying their symptoms remain unresolved. Tranquillisers and anti-depressants are also available nowadays in the bazaars of the cities and large villages in the developing countries, although here their price is so high as to put their use in effective dosage almost out of reach of the ordinary citizen.

The second interested party consists of the sufferers themselves. Our present study has only confirmed what many other field-workers have already reported, namely that psychiatric symptoms are far from rare among citizens of the developing countries, and that they are distressing enough to prompt many men and women to seek help—sometimes at considerable inconvenience and expense. A few who happen to live within reach of a doctor's clinic, a district hospital or a public health centre, may seek this help from doctors and nurses trained in Western medicine. If they do so, they are likely to receive a prescription for a psychotropic drug, only to find that they cannot afford to pay for the full course of the treatment.

The great majority of rural-dwelling citizens of developing countries are cut off from Western medical services both by distance and by their unfamiliarity with that kind of treatment. Instead, they resort to time-honoured local sources of help: to the priest of the local shrine; to a Mantarwadi or his local equivalent, a man well-versed in healing charms; or to a herbalist or other practitioner of traditional medicine. It is these traditional 'medicine-men' who constitute the third 'interested party'. For countless generations, people have consulted these rustic exorcists and healers. They do so still today throughout the Third World, and are likely to continue to do so for many years to come. Western psychiatric treatment is not available to them; in most developing countries the ratio of trained psychiatrists to the population is less than one in a million, while that of clinical psychologists or psychotherapists is even lower.

If Western psychiatric care is to reach these populations in the measurable future, it will have to be brought to them by other agents —but by whom?

Since its creation in 1948 the World Health Organisation has been dedicated to improving the quality of life in each of its member states. It has set out to achieve this by helping countries to identify and eradicate the major causes of disease, and a measure of its success has been the enormous increase in world population, which in turn brings new threats to the welfare of mankind. Today, more members of our species are being born than ever before, and a higher proportion than ever before is surviving into adult life and contributing in turn to the cumulative increase of the human race.

In celebration of its twenty-fifth anniversary, the World Health Organisation commissioned a review of the development of Basic Health Services throughout the world. This review showed that there is world-wide evidence of dissatisfaction over the failure of national health services to meet the expectations of their populations. Wide gaps have arisen between countries, and between different groups within countries, with respect to the quality of medical care available —and these gaps continue to widen still further. In all countries health care facilities are better in towns than in country districts; and this discrepancy is most marked in the developing countries where 80 per cent or more of the population are still rural dwellers. (WHO, 1973).

Hitherto, WHO has relied on the medical profession, together with its auxiliaries, to provide better medical care for the mass of mankind; but a compelling social factor has prevented these professions from advancing the general standard of basic health care to the degree that had been hoped. This factor is, quite simply, the expectation on the part of professionally trained personnel that they will enjoy a privileged position in their community with a high income and a high standard of living—which can only be achieved in modernised cities, and certainly not in the relatively spartan conditions of village life. Inevitably, doctors and skilled health professionals of all kinds are attracted by the magnetism of big-city life. For years, politicians and health planners in India, as in many other developing countries, have drawn up schemes intended to bring health care to the people, through a wide network of small-town and village Primary Health Centres; but the appeal of economic and professional self-advancement in the cities proves so strong that these fine schemes have been very imperfectly realised. Many Primary Health Centres exist only on paper, while many others are short of staff.

In 1973, two-thirds of all the doctors in Indonesia worked in the capital city of Jakarta, which housed less than one-twentieth of their country's population: in India, the great cities of Calcutta, Bombay, Delhi and Madras have also swallowed up a disproportionate number of doctors.

This concentration in the cities and large towns is still more marked in the case of specialists, such as psychiatrists, who are almost without exception city-based because only there do they find hospital appointments—and the clientele to support their private practice.

To make matters worse, young doctors, nurses and psychologists in India, as in many other developing countries, find that their career prospects will suffer if they specialise in psychiatry: senior positions are few, and relatively poorly rewarded. As a result, many of those who have received specialist training in Britain, the U.S.A. or Canada, despair of finding satsifying work in their own country and join the 'brain drain' to the West. There are, today, more psychiatrists from India, Pakistan, Bangladesh and Ceylon employed in the West than in their own respective countries. What is to be done?

Prompted by health planners in several developing countries, WHO has come to realise that the medical needs of simple, modestly-educated (or even illiterate) village people can most effectively be met by simple, modestly-trained basic health workers who themselves feel at home in rural surroundings. A pioneering work in the area, emanating from East Africa in 1966, was the book *Medical Care in Developing Countries*, edited by Dr Maurice King, in which clear statements were made about the actual tasks which have to be performed at the village level in such fields as sanitation, health education, midwifery, maternal and child health, minor trauma and sepsis, intestinal infections, etc.

In subsequent years, Dr King and his co-workers have developed the concept of the 'Health Care Package' which is a type of 'do-it-yourself kit', complete with instructions and basic equipment, designed to help village-level workers to cope with most of the common forms of morbidity which they are likely to encounter. Since 1972, several teams have been at work in Indonesia, developing simply-worded manuals of instruction in different aspects of basic health care, for the guidance of these front-line workers. This has proved a very difficult task; chapters have had to be revised and rewritten over and over again before they achieved the desired level of simplicity of expression, concentrating only on essentials. Each chapter has been finally drafted in English as well as in Bahasa Indonesia, in the hope that the English version can be readily adapted, and retranslated, for use in other countries.

Among the most difficult chapters has been that dealing with the common forms of mental disorder; yet here, too, it has been found possible to give simple instruction on 'do's' and don'ts' in mental hygiene, on first-aid measures in acute crises, on simple counselling, on the administration of psychotropic drugs, and on the after-care of the mentally ill. It will be immediately apparent that these are functions which have usually been regarded as the prerogative of the psychiatrist. In 'rural psychiatry', this is no longer the case: the nurse, or basic health worker has to be entrusted with therapeutic responsibilities. He or she will indeed work under medical supervision, but for days or weeks on end, between visits to (or by) the doctor, the front-line worker will be on his own.

This system has already been shown to work. In the late 1960's, Dr Karl Schmidt, working in Sarawak, was able to establish psychiatric outposts in small, up-river hospitals; and these were conducted, during the five or six weeks between each two-day visit by the psychiatrist, by a psychiatric nurse helped only by medical orderlies (Schmidt, 1967).

At about the same time, Dr Denny Thong, who found himself in charge of the only Mental Hosptial in Bali, Indonesia, hit upon a similar idea. He stationed five of his small staff of psychiatric nurses in general hospitals in five towns situated in the outlying districts of the island. They were each visited once a month by the psychiatrist, and all five returned to the Mental Hospital on one day each month, in order to compare notes and to seek guidance about any problem cases. These 'out-station' nurses were able to offer supervision and after-care to patients discharged from the psychiatric wards; and within a few months they found themselves consulted by increasing numbers of villagers about minor, but still distressing, psychiatric symptoms. The villagers found them more approachable, and much less intimidating than the prospect of making a long journey to consult the psychiatrist at the Mental Hospital (Dean and Thong, 1972).

Similarly, Dr Egdell in Kenya and Dr Howarth in Zambia have employed Medical Assistants, General Nurses, and Nurse-Aides, who work at the district and village level, to act as case-finders and to provide psychiatric treatment under remote supervision. In Zambia, medical technicians employed in mobile teams concerned with monitoring the prolonged treatment of lepers living at home have been trained to include surveillance of medication prescribed for chronic epileptic and schizophrenic patients also living in the villages, and have performed this task satisfactorily.

These examples show that simple forms of psychiatric care *can* be brought to the villagers by medical auxiliaries of modest education, who have been taught a limited range of skills. As yet, however, such examples are few in number, and touch only a small fraction of the hundreds of millions of these rural populations.

In India, early in 1971, an International Workshop sponsored by the World Federation for Mental Health addressed itself to the need for new techniques of delivery of mental health care; and within weeks of this meeting a gathering of senior psychiatrists and health administrators, meeting in New Delhi under the auspices of WHO, drew up a report on the Organisation and Future Needs of the

Mental Health Services in India (WHO, 1971).

The recommendations of these two groups of experts had many features in common: both groups were aware of the great disparity between the size of the problem of unmet psychiatric needs and the meagre resources of trained mental health personnel, and both looked to an expansion of medical care, out beyond its base in the District Hospital, as the best way to meet these needs. In retrospect, however, it can now be seen that this type of approach will not begin to solve the problem for many, many years.

Certainly, at the core of any community mental health service there must be experts, deploying the facilities for intensive care which only a hospital can offer; but out in the field, and particularly in remote village areas, it is quite a different matter. There, the 'front-line' workers of mental health must learn to co-exist with priests, magicians and other traditional healers in whom the villagers have confidence, while indicating that for some forms of mental illness, at least, they have medicines and procedures which can powerfully supplement the ancient remedies.

In many countries, ancient and modern therapies are practised side by side, often in rivalry but sometimes in co-operation. The latter can be seen in parts of the Sudan, where two outstanding psychiatrists set a new pattern of treatment. Dr Tigani El Mahi, who was both an Arabic scholar and a London-trained specialist, set out to enlist the co-operation of the Mollahs or Moslem priests to whom the simple citizen first turns for help, especially in cases of mental derangement. He showed that he respected their knowledge of the Koran and their spiritual authority, and this encouraged them in turn to acknowledge his 'foreign' skills. In time, Dr Tigani and his able successor, Dr Taha Baasher, established a working relationship with numerous Mollahs both in Khartoum and in distant towns and villages, whereby the Mollahs learned how to recognise cases of schizophrenia and epilepsy, which could not be cured by spiritual means alone, and they would refer such cases to the psychiatrist's clinic. The psychiatrists, in turn, recognised that shared religious belief, and participation in sacred rituals, could be of great value to sufferers from neurosis and also to their own psychotic patients, following their discharge from hospital or outpatient clinic treatment.

In Nigeria, also, another psychiatrist pioneer, Dr T. A. Lambo, was the originator of the world-famous Aro Village Scheme, in which rural patients lived in familiar surroundings, and frequently continued to consult traditional medicine-men, while receiving medication under the supervision of nurses from a modern psychiatric hospital. Here, as in the Sudan, co-operation between traditional and modern healers was based on a mutual respect for each other's role, while the patient got the best of both worlds.

It would be unrealistic to pretend that this degree of co-operation is easily achieved. All too often mutual denigration and rivalry are found instead. Traditional healers accuse Western doctors and their assistants of being too mercenary; and doctors accuse them in turn of practices based on ignorance, which cause harm. It is understandable that some traditional healers should feel that their reputation, their livelihood and their spiritual authority may be undermined if Western medicines are seen to relieve patients whom they were unable to cure.

In India, there is a rather special situation, because here there is a culture which has a truly remarkable ability to tolerate contradictions. The Western antithesis of 'either-or' is replaced by the Hindu concept that many systems of belief, although seemingly incompatible, can all be true—because each represents one of the innumerable aspects of reality. Hence, at the village level, people who are ill or in trouble think it perfectly natural to consult not one, but several sources of help; both authors of this book have often had the experience of treating village patients while being well aware that before the day was out they would visit a temple in order to make a vow, and then perhaps consult a Mantarwadi about the same complaint. Among their most highly educated and 'Westernised' fellow-countrymen it is quite usual to find scientifically trained physicians —or atomic physicists—who readily admit to belief in the supernatural.

In such an all-embracing culture, one might expect to find many examples of the co-existence of traditional and modern forms of therapy; they certainly do co-exist, in the patients' own experience, but this seldon finds expression in deliberate co-operation between the different kinds of healer—and yet there are some outstanding exceptions. Two of these can be found in the field of psychiatry, in the persons of Dr Vidya Sagar and Dr N. C. Surya.

In the early 1950s, Dr Vidya Sagar assumed charge of an old, overcrowded mental hospital in the outskirts of the city of Amritsar. Here, four thousand patients were crudely tended by a very small staff of doctors and nurses, assisted by men and women attendants of rudimentary education. When he arrived on the scene, outpatient treatment was negligible—some 200 patients a year. Relatives brought severely ill patients, for whom every traditional remedy had been tried in vain, in order to abandon them for ever behind the closed confines of the 'mad-house'.

Dr Vidya Sagar's first reform was to urge the relatives to stay for a time. He pitched tents within the hospital grounds to accomodate them, and encouraged them to feed and tend the sick member of their family—and thereby at once greatly improved his patients' nutrition and nursing care. His next move was to assemble large groups of relatives, sometimes as many as 200 at a time, and to conduct an informal case conference in which he drew upon their own recent experience to teach them about the symptoms of the psychoses, about treatment, and about the ways in which their behaviour towards a patient could help or aggravate his or her condition. In these harangues, Dr Vidya Sagar drew freely upon his knowledge of classic Hindu religious tests, the very style of his address resembling that of a Hindu holy man offering *satsang*, or religious enlightenment. He also worked prodigiously long hours— often far past midnight—in order to deal personally with the scores of patients and their families who waited all day in order to have an audience with him; and he refused to accept any payment other than his modest governmental salary. Not surprisingly he came to be regarded in Amritsar, and in villages for many miles around, as a saintly person, devoted to the service of others, in the tradition of Mahatma Gandhi or Vinoba Bhave. His hospital completely changed its character: instead of being a closed, rather stagnant community it became renowned as a place to visit and re-visit. Each year, more than 9000 outpatients attended for treatment, while the turnover of inpatients, accompanied by their relatives, also increased greatly. All this was accomplished in the apparently unpromising surroundings of a hundred-year-old mental hospital; and yet the greatest change brought about was not so much the revitalisation of the hospital as a comunity mental health centre— important though that was—as Dr Vidya Sagar's enlistment of many thousands of relatives as village-level helpers, better informed and better equipped than before to take care of mentally disturbed members of their family or their village.

Dr Vidya Sagar's blend of Western psychiatry and Hindu religious teaching developed over half a life-time. In striking contrast was the experience of Dr N. C. Surya, the former Director of the All-India Institute of Mental Health in Bangalore. Dr Surya's medical career had included several years as an army doctor and several more spent in Europe, where he not only completed his training in psychiatry but also mastered German and Russian so that he could study their contributions to this speciality as well as those of the English-speaking world. When he took up his very responsible post in Bangalore he believed that social, political and economic changes were no less important than the provision of treatment services, if the level of mental health of India's impoverished peasants and labourers were to be improved.

During his few years as Director, however, he found himself seriously questioning the Marxist dialectical materialism which had greatly attracted him during his years in the West. Instead, he returned to the practice of meditation and to the study of the Bhagavadgita, the Vedas and the Puranas, classic Hindu texts in which he found many profound observations on normal and abnormal human psychology. Quite suddenly, in the summer of 1968, he abandoned his academic position and surrendered his wordly possessions to the Sri Aurobindo Ashram in Pondicherry, where he has lived ever since with his wife and family. He continues to practise psychiatry both in the Ashram and in charitable village dispensaries; and meanwhile he treats his numerous visitors to discussions of the relevance of Hindu religious philosophy to current problems in mental health. His professional colleagues wait expectantly for the publication of his thoughts on this topic.

It is a commonplace to say that every developing country is experiencing rapid social change. Economically, they are trying to emulate the industrialised countries, whether they model themselves on capitalist, or socialist or (in most cases) on mixed economies; politically, they all claim to be democracies, although the term has been variously interpreted in the Philippines, in Indonesia, in Thailand and in Nepal—as indeed, it has been in different Western countries. Social changes are also taking place, but at a slower rate. There is a real danger, which social planners have not always succeeded in avoiding, in these countries' trying to emulate the medical and social services of a 'Welfare State' before they have achieved the economic basis required to implement such plans.

Here, it is instructive to compare two Eastern countries in one of which major political and economic changes took place just over half a century ago, in the other, just over a quarter-century ago. These are the Mongolian People's Republic, and the People's Republic of China, respectively. In the former, the mainstay of the economy is still the tending of vast herds of horses, camels, cattle, sheep and goats. Industrialisation is still largely confined to two cities, and the bulk of the population is spread thinly over vast areas of pastures, mountains and deserts. The visitor to Mongolia, especially one who is familiar with the countries of South-East Asia, is at once impressed by four things: by the evident social equality of all Mongolian citizens; by their high standard of nutrition; by their achievement of universal basic education, and by a medical service which reaches right out into the population.

The front-line workers of this service are the Feldschers, men and women whose training is mid-way between that of a doctor and that of a nurse. Even remote communities of nomadic herdsmen are visited, either on horseback or by motor-bicycle, by a Feldscher who has responsibility (as does a Western General Practitioner) for a population of 2000 to 2500 persons. When necessary, the Feldscher can summon an ambulance or a light airplane to convey a patient to the nearest 100-bedded District Hospital; but for most of the time they are on their own.

Here, as in any other country, neurotic illness often presents with physical symptoms. In the 'neuropsychiatric' wards of their District Hospitals one can find many patients who would be regarded by a Western-trained doctor as suffering from psychosomatic disorders; but here the neuropsychiatrist (whose training reflects, at second-hand, what was orthodox training in Moscow thirty years ago, just as the teaching in English-medium medical schools of the East often encapsulates that of an earlier generation of teachers in London or Edinburgh) confidently diagnoses 'neurasthenia' or 'nervous debility' and prescribes cupping, or injections of vitamins, or prolonged sleep as appropriate treatment. It is apparent that a basic level of care in physical illness has been made available to the mass of the predominantly rural population; but the common emotionally-determined disabilities remain relatively neglected.

In Mao's China, the adaptation of an ancient predominantly peasant society to socialism has been marked by a deliberate refusal slavishly to imitate Western institutions. Accepting the need to move step by step in the process of industrialisation, which is essential if they are to succeed in raising their standard of living, they have seen the advantage of developing 'intermediate technology', that is, small-scale factories and partial mechanisation of the work in the fields. They have set out to prevent the drift towards the cities, characteristic of so many developing countries, by bringing amenities equal to city life to the large rural village-communes. The provision of a similar, though very basic, standard of health care for workers in town and country has been part of this process of equalisation.

China differs from most other developing countries in that front-line medical care is *not* provided by health professionals—not by doctors, nor feldschers, nor nurses, nor any other full-time medical auxiliaries, but by their celebrated 'barefoot doctors' who remain working members of their agricultural or industrial communes and practise a homely form of district nursing in their spare time. Like members of certain voluntary organisations such as the Red Cross, the Red Crescent or the St. John's Ambulance Brigade, they never cease to be ordinary 'lay' members of the community which they serve; and like them, they attend short courses of training, followed at intervals by refresher courses in order to improve their skills. Side by side with the 'barefoot doctors', who can enlist the help of more highly trained, hospital-based nurses and doctors when they encounter difficult cases, there are also village healers versed in traditional herbal remedies and in the technique of acupuncture; but these, too, are 'workers' first and only engaged part-time in healing.

China became a full participant in the World Health Organisation only in 1972, at the very time when WHO was carrying out its re-appraisal of the delivery of health care in the Third World. Conse-quently, international health planners have shown a lively interest in their method of providing better care at the grass-roots level, throughout their vast population. Not least of their innovations has been their demonstration that an acceptable level of first-line health care can be given in the absence of doctors, nurses or hospitals, thus keeping those most costly resources to deal with more serious con-ditions, where their skills are essential.

Visitors to the People's Republic of China have been greatly impressed by the appropriateness and efficiency of this basic level of health care; but as yet we have had very little information about how perceptive citizens of the new China are of neurotic and psycho-somatic disorders, or about their attitudes towards more seriously mentally ill patients in their midst.

Ideally, any system which offers basic health care at the grass-roots level should include the recognition of common forms of mental ill-health, and should offer appropriate supportive care for some, while invoking more specialised attention for the more seriously ill. As yet, no country in the world has fully realised so balanced a pattern of care in its health services; almost invariably provision for mental health care lags behind the rest of the service, and this is conspicuously the case in every developing country. Yet, a balanced provision is what we should aim for; and only by experi-menting in field situations, with village-level workers who have been taught at least first-aid measures in mental health care, will this age-old neglect of mental suffering begin to be overcome.

The present study has shown that psychiatric symptoms severe enough to cause significant amounts of incapacity and distress are common in a rural Indian community. The next stage must be to plan practical methods of meeting these needs and to test their efficacy in pilot trials before recommending their adoption on a wider scale. Being ourselves neither saints nor politicians, but social psychiatrists, the authors of this book believe that ultimately it will be a responsibility of each country's health and social services, working in collaboration, to respond to these needs.

The present study has demonstrated the high level of prevalence of psychiatric symptoms in a South Indian rural community. Roughly one adult in three admitted to one or more of such symptoms at the time of our survey, but by no means all of these people were seriously incommoded by their symptoms. On the other hand, those who had two or more symptoms were very likely to report that they were handicapped by them, so that they could no longer cope normally with their work and their social relationships. A majority of those with two or more symptoms had taken the trouble to seek assistance because of them from a doctor or from a village healer; out of the population surveyed, 8 per cent were in this category. A slightly smaller number, 6 per cent of the total, scored at the highest point on our 'Need Scale'; that is, they reported four or more symptoms, had consulted someone for help, and declared themselves unable to cope because of their symptoms.

6 per cent of the adult population of India represents nearly 18 million people in need of help. The size of the problem almost boggles the imagination, especially when one recalls the very limited resources of mental health personnel. Usually, at this point, one gratefully acknowledges the persistence of traditional sources of support, in the extended family, the Mantarwadi, the Patri and their similars in different parts of Village India. Our study, however, has thrown up a number of reminders that Indian culture is no longer static, but changing. For example, we found that the agency of first choice for the treatment of a number of conditions, including all those with psychotic symptoms, was the clinic of a Western-trained doctor.

The village of Kota was typical of only a minority of Indian villages, in having a dispensary with such a doctor actually there in its midst. Most villagers live many miles away from the nearest clinic. No doubt this was why, both in response to our attitude survey and in their observed behaviour, so many Kota people showed an awareness of the help which could be given by allopathic medicines. At the same time, they had recourse, as do their fellow-countrymen in hundreds of thousands of smaller villages, to a variety of other sources of help.

Following the lead of WHO, health planners in India, as in other countries, are studying methods of employing modestly trained 'Primary Health Workers'—men and women recruited from the rural population itself—to carry out simple tasks of health education and basic health care. Our Indian colleagues in the field of Mental Health have been urging that such village-level workers should be enlisted to help in the recognition and treatment of at least some of the most pressing needs for mental health care also—if only for the epileptics and schizophrenics whose existence can be made much easier by the regular administration of readily available drugs.

In September 1974, colleagues from India took part in an Expert Committee, at WHO headquarters in Geneva, in which psychiatrists and health planners from all the major developing countries addressed themselves to this problem (WHO, 1975). As in all such planning sessions, however, this Committee was compelled to recognise the enormous discrepancies which exist between the multitude of those in need of help and the small numbers of trained personnel. Its report acknowledged that for many years to come most sufferers from minor mental disorders in developing countries would continue to seek help from traditional healers; the task of the Mental Health Services must be carried out through the spreading general health clinics, staffed by doctors and nurses at the Primary Health Centre level, and by more modestly trained workers at the village level. Mental Health workers would offer a back-up service of treatment for the most difficult cases, and of consultation for front-line workers who would themselves treat many such cases in the course of their daily work.

At this very moment, a completely new approach to the whole problem of health care has been enunciated—although as yet only in broad and sweeping terms—by the world-famous social philosopher, Ivan Illich. In a book entitled *Medical Nemesis*, published late in 1974, he has urged the 'de-professionalization' of health care. He argues that by surrendering the responsibility for the maintenance of health and the cure of illness to the medical profession, people all over the world have done themselves a grave disservice. This is not to deny the great advances of medical science; but he does seriously question the wisdom of handing over to others tasks which should be the concern of individuals, families and communities. Illich reminds us that even today the majority of episodes of illness are self-limiting conditions, relatively uninfluenced by medical intervention; he deplores the assumption, already prevalent throughout the Western countries, that pain and illness are to be regarded as 'unnatural' experiences from which doctors are expected to release every sufferer as quickly as possible. Western doctors share in this mistaken belief, that there must be a medicinal remedy for every ailment, and as a result of over-zealous prescribing iatrogenic illnesses (which are themselves the consequence of medical intervention) are becoming increasingly numerous—nowhere more so than in the U.S.A.

The remedy which Illich proposes is that individuals and communities should re-assume responsibility for their health, and for the health of their environment. He would like to see ordinary citizens sharing in the provision of sound hygiene, adequate nutrition and treatment of common illnesses for themselves and their neighbours. He points out that most demonstrably effective medical treatments have two characteristics: they are relatively cheap, and their administration can be taught to any reasonably intelligent person.

In the Western countries, the medical profession has a very strong vested interest in controlling health care; and yet already public expectations are outstripping the doctors' ability to meet the demands placed upon them. As a result, in one Western country after another, nurses, pharmacists, social workers and other 'para-professionals' are becoming increasingly engaged in therapy. In the developing countries, where doctors are scarce, this delegation of the doctor's role is proceeding even more rapidly; but in neither of these areas are the citizens themselves enlisted in the tasks of health preservation to the degree that Illich advocates. In spite of their lower standards of education, the societies of the Third World have one great advantage, in the strength of their kinship and community groups, which have never lost their functions of self-help and mutual help; all they need is to learn the use of those tools which medical science can now put at their disposal.

Throughout this discussion it has been taken for granted that mental health is an integral part of health in general. Interruptions in people's ability to cope with their normal tasks, and interruptions in individuals' 'feeling well' may be due to injuries, infections or other forms of organic dysfunction; but they also can be due—in South Indian villagers, no less than in the Western world—to anxieties, fears, or troubled interpersonal relationships.

In the West, these temporary spells of 'not being able to cope' are sometimes treated by psychotherapy, more often palliated by prescriptions of tranquillising drugs. Psychotherapy has this in common with many forms of traditional 'magical' healing, that it helps the individual to regain his own autonomy, and his ability to relate to his fellow-men. In contrast, there are some more serious forms of mental disorder, such as epilepsy and the psychoses, in which modern drugs can contribute significantly to the patient's relief, if not to his recovery. Here, as in other forms of health care, the challenge which is going to face the professionals, especially in the developing countries, during the next generation will be to discover how to share knowledge and treatment skills as widely as possible with the members of the vast populations which they have to serve.

In countries like India, the role of psychiatrists and their co-workers—who will include doctors, nurses, social workers and psychologists and also, it may be hoped, other mental health aides drawn from the local community—will be to supplement rather than to rival the helping agencies which still operate, as they have done for centuries, in the rural way of life. The present study has revealed both the villagers' loyalty to their traditional healers, and their readiness to make use of new knowledge and new remedies whenever these prove demonstrably helpful.

If, as yet, this concept of the sharing of psychological insight, and of modern therapies, with peoples who still maintain a very different world-view and system of ideas seems somewhat utopian and unlikely of realisation, we take comfort in the fact that we have seen radical changes in health care come about during our own lifetimes. This encourages us to hope that we may yet live to see the relief of mental disorders—which are so frequent, although seldom recognised, in the peoples of the developing countries—incorporated in a new blend of traditional and modern approaches to the preservation of physical and mental health in the Third World.

APPENDIX I

EDINBURGH—MANIPAL
PSYCHIATRIC RESEARCH PROJECT
INDIAN PSYCHIATRIC
SURVEY SCHEDULE*

SECTION 1: PRELIMINARY INQUIRY

Identification No:
Name:
Address:

Introduction: We are trying to assess the health status of the people in this area, with a view to helping those who are not well. We are inquiring not only about the illnesses of the body, but also about mental problems. I shall ask you a few questions now. If anything is not clear, please do not hesitate to ask. All right?

Sub-Section 1: Social and Demographic data

1. Caste: 0 = Brahmin   1 = Bant   2 = Moger

2. Age:

3. Sex: 0 = Male   1 = Female

4. Education:
0 = Nil	5 = Pre-university
1 = 3 R's	6 = Degree
2 = Primary	7 = Postgraduate
3 = Middle	8 = Any other training after
4 = Secondary	school

5. Main occupation:
0 = Land owner	7 = Student
1 = Tenant	8 = Housewife
2 = Agricultural labour	9 = Other
3 = Fisherman	Y = None
4 = Business	If 'Other', please specify:
5 = Professional	. . . .
6 = Services (non-professional)	. . . .

6. Income in units:
   - 0 = less than 200
   - 1 = 201–400
   - 2 = 401–600
   - 3 = 601–800
   - 4 = 801–1000
   - 5 = 1001 and above

---

* This is the English version of the Kannada schedule used in the Kota survey.

7. Marital status: 0 = Single   5 = Remarried
                     1 = Married   6 = More than one wife
                     2 = Separated   7 = Other
                     3 = Divorced
                     4 = Widowed

8. Family: 0 = Joint   1 = Unitary   2 = Single

9. Family members: 0 = less than 3   1 = 4–6
                     2 = 7–9   3 = 10–12
                     4 = 13–15   5 = 16 or more

10. Subject's age at   X = Not known   1 = 6–15
    father's death: Y = Not applicable   2 = 16–20
                        0 = Below 5   3 = 21 +

11. Subject's age at   X = Not known   1 = 6–15
    mother's death: Y = Not applicable   2 = 16–20
                        0 = Below 5   3 = 21 +

12. Consanguinity in   Y = Not known   1 = Present
    parents: 0 = Absent

13. Inheritance: 0 = Patrilineal   1 = Matrilineal

14. Living with spouse: 0 = less than 3 months   1 = 3–6 months
                        2 = more than 6 months, in past year

Sub-Section 2: Physical Symptoms

Q.1   How is your health? Are you physically ill in any way? (Any pain, burning, itching, numbness in any part of the body? Any dizziness, nausea, bowel trouble, urine trouble? Since when? How often during the last one month?)

Q.2   Have you been feeling weak or tired lately? (Even when you are not working?) (Since when? How often during the last one month?)

Q.3   Do you suffer from fits or attacks of unconsciousness? (Since when? How often during the last one year?)

	Head	Chest	Anogenital	Rest/whole body
* Pain	....	....	....	....
* Burning	....	....	....	....
* Itching	....	....	....	....
* Numbness	....	....	....	....
* Other odd sensations	....	....	....	....
Other sensations/ Specify	....	....	....	....
	....	....	....	....

* Dizziness   * Indigestion   * Weakness

* Nausea   * Wind   * Fits

* If other illness, please specify.......................................   ....

....

Sub-Section 3: Sleep and appetite

Q.4 How is your sleep these days? Do you sleep well? *If no:*

Q. What is wrong with your sleep? .... Is it that you take a long time to go to sleep? .... or is it that you wake up too early? .... or is it that your sleep is disturbed through the night?

If sleep delay:

Q. Since when? How often during the last week? (How long do you take to sleep once you are in bed? .... and before?) (Once asleep, do you sleep through the night quite well?)

If early waking:

Q. Since when? How often during the last week? (What time do you get up in the morning? .... and before?)

If disturbed sleep throughout the night:

Q. Since when? How often during the last week? (How long do you keep awake during the night? .... and before?) (Do you sleep at all?) (Do you wake up a number of times?)

Q.5 Do you get terrifying dreams which wake you up during the night? (Since when? How often during the last week?) (What happens when you wake up? Do you get palpitation, sweating, tremors, etc.?)

     Sleep delay   *Generalized sleeplessness*
     Early waking   *Nightmares*

Q.6 How is your appetite these days? Do you eat well?

     Loss of appetite

Sub-Section 4: Memory, concentration, etc.

Q.7 Is your memory all right? Do you find it difficult to remember things? (Since when? Was your memory all right before?) (What sort of things do you forget? Can you give an example?)

Q.8 Some people find it difficult to concentrate on what is going on: when they are working or when someone is talking to them, their mind tends to fly away. Have you any such problem? (Since when? Was your concentration good before?) (Can you give an example?)

     Subjective forgetfulness   *Poor concentration*

Sub-Section 5: Worries, anxiety, tension, etc.

Q.9 All of us have some worries. Is there anything especially worrying you these days? (Your work, financial condition, home, spouse, children, relatives?)

If yes:

Q. Tell me more about it. What is it exactly bothering you about ....?

Q. What is it like when you worry? Do unpleasant thoughts go round and round in your head? (Do you find it difficult to push those thoughts out of your mind?)

     Pathological worrying:
     About ....

Q.10 Some people have the habit of comparing themselves with others, and worrying that they are not as good as others .... in work or conversation or looks for example. Do you get any such thoughts? (In what way do you feel inferior to others?) (Do such thoughts trouble you a lot? Do you find it difficult to push them out once they come?)

Feelings of inferiority:
About ....

Q.11 Some people get very anxious or afraid under certain conditions: for example, in the dark, when they are alone, or when they have to talk to strangers, or when they have to travel alone. Do you have any fears of this kind? (What situations make you afraid?) (Do you *always* feel anxious when in this situation?) (Do you get any thumping of the heart, sweating or trembling of hands when in this situation?) (Do you try to avoid such situations? Always? Can you give an example?)

Q.12 (a) Do you sometimes feel anxious or afraid without reason?
     (b) Do you sometimes get thumping of the heart, sweating or trembling of the hands without reason?
     (Since when? How often during the last week?) (Can you give an example?)

Situational anxiety   Phobias   Freefloating anxiety
Situational anxiety in...
Phobia of..

If situational anxiety, phobia or freefloating anxiety present:

Q. Have there been times when you felt so afraid that you had to scream for help or run away? (How often during the last month?) (Can you give an example?)

   Panic attacks:

Q.13 Do you sometimes feel that your body is tense, your muscles are taut, and your nerves are being pulled? (Since when? How often during the last week?) (Can you give an example?)

   Muscular tension:

Q.14 Do you sometimes feel very restless, so much so that you cannot keep still? (Since when? How often during the last week?) (Can you give an example?)

   Restlessness:

If restlessness present:

Q. Have you ever felt so restless that you wanted to leave everything and just go away? (From your home, your work, from everything?) (How often have you felt like this during the last month?) (Have you had these feelings before?) (Can you give an example?) (Have you actually run away at any time?)

   Fugitive impulse: *Running away:*

Q.15 Have you ever felt that there are too many thoughts in your mind and they keep pressing on you? (Since when? How often during the last week?) (Can you give an example?) (What kind of thoughts?) *If no:*

Q. Have you ever felt that you cannot think properly, and that your mind becomes blank and empty? (Since when? How often during the last week? (Can you give an example?) (What do you think this is due to?)

   Pressure of ideas: ·   *Poverty of thought:*

Q.16 Do you feel very irritable at times for minor reasons? (Since when? How often during the last week?) (Can you give an example?)

   Irritability:

(From this point onwards, in the interests of brevity, the details of wording of the questions have been omitted, with a few exceptions.)

Sub-Section 6: Mood

Q.17-21 Relate to symptoms of:
Depression
Loss of interest
Suicidal feeling
* Guilt feelings
Dullness
Feelings of incompetence
* Suicidal attempt
Self blame

Sub-Section 7: Obsessions and compulsions

Q.22 and 23 relate to:
* Compulsions
* Obsessional ideas ·

Sub-Section 8: Sexual problems

Q.24 is worded differently for unmarried male, unmarried female and for spouses and relates to:
* Sexual problems
Painful menstruation

Sub-Section 9: Delusions and hallucinations

Q.25-29 relate to:
* Demon trouble
* Hallucinations
* Ideas of persecution
* Special powers

Note I: Refer for detailed examination in Section II, Sub section 1, if:
(a) any starred symptom is present
(b) subject is unco-operative
(c) you have noticed odd behaviour during conversation
(d) when the speech of the subject is not understandable

Note II: Refer the person for detailed history and examination of social functioning, if any symptom is present.

Note III: Refer the person for detailed examination, if he has been mentioned in Sub Section 10, below.

Sub-Section 10: Questions about others

Introduction: I have asked so many questions about yourself. Now a few more questions about others. In your family or neighbours or friends, is there anyone:

1 Who is admitted to Mental Hospital?

2 Who is mad, talks nonsense and acts in a strange manner?

3 Who suffers from fits or loss of conciousness?

4 Who has become very quiet and does not talk to people?

5 Who claims to hear voices or see things others cannot hear or see?

6 Who is very suspicious and claims that some people are trying to harm him?

7 Who has become unusually cheerful, makes jokes and brags that he is a big man, when he is not really so?

8 Who has become sad lately, and cries without reason?

9 Who has lost his memory, or is losing his memory?

10 Who has always from birth been stupid or dull like a child?

11 Who has tried to commit suicide?

12 Who actually committed suicide?

13 Who gets possessed by bhutas and spirits?

14 Who is lazy and does not work, though physically healthy?

15 Who drinks too much or gambles too much or has other bad habits?

SECTION II: DETAILED INQUIRY FROM THE SUBJECT

Note: This Section should be completed by a trained Psychiatrist only.

Sub Section 1: Details about reported symptoms

1 *If specified physical symptoms have been reported,* ask the details of the illness and conduct a general physical examination. Determine the likelihood or not, of physical illness.

Liklihood of physical illness:

Y = No physical symptom
0 = Physical illness likely
1 = Physical illness unlikely
2 = Undetermined, further investigation necessary

If physical illness unlikely:

Q. Are you much worried about your health? (Do the thoughts about your health go round and round in your head?) (Do you find it difficult to push these thoughts out of your mind?) (What do you think might happen because of these symptoms?)

Hypochondriacal preoccupation

2 *If the subject complains of paralysis, loss of sensation, loss of co-ordination, blindness, deafness, aphonia or any other symptom which came on suddenly, does not fit the neurological pattern, and seems to be 'suspect' in any other way,* conduct a neurological examination and note whether any of the following conditions are present:

Hysterical paralysis
Hysterical parasthesia
Hysterical ataxia
Hysterical blindness
Hysterical deafness
Hysterical aphonia
Hysterical conversion (other)

If other, please specify: ....

3 *If the subject complains of fits,* conduct the detailed questioning in the presence of a near relative who has seen at least one fit.

Questions are asked about the frequency and characteristics of the fit, enabling the investigator to rate them as:

Epileptic or
Hysterical

4 *If the subject complains of sexual problems:*

For unmarried males: Four questions, with supplementaries, relating to:

Sexual preoccupation
Masturbation worries
Night emission worries
Other sexual problems

For married males: Four questions, with supplementaries, relating to:

Loss of sexual desire
Impotence
Premature ejaculation
Other sexual problems

For married females:
Note: Conduct this questioning through a female investigator.

Two questions, with supplementaries, relating to:

Loss of sexual desire
Other sexual problems

5 *If subject reports guilt feelings:*

Q. You say you have harmed someone. Can you tell me more about it? (Do you feel you have committed a sin for which you should be punished? What sin: What should the punishment be?)

Delusions of guilt:

Description of delusions:

6 *If subject reports attempted suicide:* questions are asked relating to:

Number of occasions
Date of last occasion
Method employed
Reason

7 *If possession reported,* conduct the detailed questioning in the presence of a near relative who has seen *at least one attack.*

Q. You say you get possessed by demons. How often have you been possessed during the last year? (What happens during the possession?) (How long does it last?) (How is the demon taken away?)

Possession state:

Description of possession state:

8 *If any other trouble by demons and spirits:*

Q. You say you have been troubled by demons and spirits. What do they do? Can you tell me about it? (Why are they doing it?) (What have you done about this trouble?)

Delusion: *Supernatural persecution:*

Description of delusion:

9 *If enemies reported:*

Q.   You say that you have enemies. What do they say to you? (Do you find that people talk about you? How do you know?) (Has anyone tried to cast spells on you?) (Is anyone trying to poison you in any way?) (Who is it/are they? Why is he/are they doing it?) (What have you done about it?)

> *Ideas of reference:*
> *Delusion, human persecution:*
>
> *Description of delusion:*

10   *If spiritual powers or other special powers claimed:*

Q.   You say you have special powers. What are they? (How did you get them?) (Have you ever used them?) (Do you think you are an important person or related to some important person?)

> *Grandiose delusions:*
>
> *Description of Delusion:*

11   *If claim made to hear or see things others cannot hear or see:*

Five questions, with supplementaries, relating to:

> *Auditory hallucinations:*
> *Visual hallucinations:*
> *Olfactory hallucinations:*
> *Gustatory hallucinations:*
> *Tactile hallucinations:*
>
> *Description of hallucinations:*

Sub-Section 2: History of present illness

Q.1   Elicits order of occurence of symptoms noted.

Q.2   Elicits duration of symptoms.

Q.3 and supplementaries, elicits course of the disorder, over time:

Q.4   What do you think is the main cause of your troubles?

> *Cause of trouble:* X = Not known
>   0 = Hereditary factors
>   1 = Bereavement
>   2 = Financial loss
>   3 = Family quarrels
>   4 = Failure in business/work/exam
>   5 = Sudden fright
>   6 = Spirits/Ghosts
>   7 = Spells
>   8 = Failure in love affair
>   9 = Other

If other, please specify: ....

Q.5   Elicits history of consultation with:

> *Allopathic doctor*
> *Ayurvedic doctor*
> *Psychiatrist/mental hospital*
> *Astrologer*
> *Medium*
> *Temple*
> *Family elders*
> *Other*

If other, please specify: ....

Q.6   Elicits previous history of mental illness:

     Description:

Q.7   Previous attempts at suicide.

Q.8   Family history of mental illness:

     Description:

SECTION III: DETAILED INQUIRY FROM A NEAR RELATIVE

Note I: This Section should be completed by a trained Psychiatrist, when:

     (a) any symptom has been reported in Sub Section 10 of the Preliminary Inquiry;

     (b) detailed inquiry with the subject shows the presence of delusions/ hallucinations/possession states/fits;

     (c) the interviewer on the preliminary inquiry has noticed something odd about the subject's speech, behaviour or mood.

Note II: The Section should be completed by interviewing a near relative who sees the subject at least one hour a day. If the subject is a vagrant, interview should be conducted with an informed person of the area. If the person who first reported the symptom(s) qualifies under the criteria laid down, the detailed inquiry may be conducted with him directly.

Sub-Section 1: Symptoms

Q.1   How is his sleep? Does he sleep well? *If yes:*

Q.   Does he sleep more than usual by any chance? (How do you know? Can you give an example?) (Since when? How often during the last week?) *If reduced sleep:*

Q.   Is it that he takes a long time to go to sleep?.... or is it that he wakes up too early? .... or is his sleep disturbed throughout the night? (How do you know? Can you give an example?) (Since when? How often during the last week?)

Q.1 and supplementaries, relate to:

     Oversleeping
     Early waking
     Sleep delay
     Generalised sleeplessness

Q.2 and 3 and supplementaries, relate to:

     Increased appetite
     Decreased appetite

Q.4-7 relate to:

     Irritability
     Abusiveness
     Violence

Q.8 and supplementaries:

     Suspiciousness
     Depression
     Elation

Q.9 and 10 relate to:

> *Too much speech*
> *Too little speech*
> *Muteness*
> *Non-understandable speech*

Q.11 Does he ever say that someone is trying to harm him whem no-one really is? (Can you give an example?)

Q.12 Does he ever say that some spirit has entered his body? (Can you give an example?)

Q.13 Does he say that he is being troubled by spirits/bhutas in any other way? (Can you give an example?)

Q.14 Does he say he has special powers or that he is related to important people when it is not true? (Can you give an example?)

Q.15 Does he say he has committed a great sin, for which he should be punished, when it is not true? (Can you give an example?)

Q.16 Does he express any other strange ideas of this sort? (Can you give an example?)

Q.11–17 relate to:

> *Delusions of persecution: human*
> *Possession state*
> *Delusions of persecution: supernatural*
> *Delusions of grandeur*
> *Delusions of guilt*
> *Other delusions*
> *Hallucinations*

Q.18–22 relate to:

> *Loss of memory*
> *Disorientation*
> *Lack of self-care*
> *Complete dependence*

If lack of self-care absent, questions are asked relating to:

> *Reduced capacity to work*
> *Social withdrawal*
> *Oversociability*
> *Increased religiosity*
> *Reduced religiosity*

Sub-Section 2: History of present illness

Note: Omit the following questions if none of the symptoms in Sub Section 1 are present:

Q.1   Order of recurrence of symptoms: ....

Q.2, 3, and supplementaries:

> *Duration of illness*
> *Mode of onset*
> *Course*
> *Outcome*

Q.4   Believed cause of trouble:

Q.5   History of consultation with:

> *Allopathic doctor*
> *Ayurvedic doctor*
> *Psychiatrist/Mental Hospital*
> *Astrologer*
> *Medium*
> *Temple*
> *Family elders*
> *Other*

If other, please specify: ....

Q.6   Previous history of mental illness

Q.7   Previous history of attempted suicide

Q.8   Family history of mental illness

Q.9   Family history of suicide

SECTION IV: OBSERVATION

Note: This Section should be completed by a trained Psychiatrist, if delusion and/or hallucinations have been detected in Section II, or when a symptom has been recorded in Section III. He records presence of any of the following:

Slowness and underactivity	....	*Histrionic*	....
Restlessness	....	*Too much speech*	....
Excitement	....	*Too little speech*	....
Bizarre behaviour	....	*Mutism*	....
Excessive preoccupation	....	*Incoherent speech*	....
Distractability	....	*Irrelevant speech*	....
Stupor	....	*Flight of ideas*	....
Echopraxia	....	*Persecutory delusions*	....
Negativism	....	*Grandiose delusions*	....
Ambitendence	....	*Delusions of possession*	....
Flexibilitas cerea	....	*Delusions of guilt*	....
Echolalia	....	*Other delusions*	....
Blunted effect	....	*Auditory hallucinations*	....
Incongruous effect	....	*Visual hallucinations*	....
Hostile irritability	....	*Other hallucinations*	....
Hypomanic mood	....	*Delirium*	....
		Disorientation	....

Q.1–4 Disorientation

SECTION V: DETAILED INQUIRY ABOUT SOCIOPATHIC ITEMS

Note I: This Section should be completed if the subject has been reported to consume too much alcohol or have other bad habits distressing to those around him.

Note II: The Section should be completed by interviewing a near relative who sees the subject at least one hour every day. If the subject is a vagrant, interview should be conducted with an informed person of the area. If the person who first reported the symptom(s) qualifies under the criteria laid down, the detailed inquiry may be conducted with him directly.

Sub Section 1: Symptoms

Q.1   Abuse of alcohol

Q.2   Abuse of drugs

Q.3   Anti-social habits

  Description:

Q.4 and supplementaries:

  Lack of self-care
  Complete dependence

  If lack of self-care absent, questions are asked relating to:

  Reduced capacity to work
  Social withdrawal
  Oversociability
  Reduced religiosity
  Increased religiosity

A glossary of symptoms and their definitions

To ensure inter-investigator reliability, it is imperative that the different researchers use similar criteria for deciding whether a symptom is to be recorded as present or not. An attempt is made in this Section to provide such criteria through standard definitions for each of the symptoms mentioned in the Schedule. Some definitions will appear to be purely arbitrary. For example, no logical reason can be given why sleep delay should be recorded when it has occurred 'at least twice' during the preceding week, and not 'at least thrice' or 'only once'. Such rigid directions can, however, be justified on the grounds that clear, standard criteria should be available to the researchers.

The definitions must be adhered to strictly. Except when specified otherwise, a symptom will be recorded only when it has been present at least twice during the week preceding the interview.

SECTION I: PRELIMINARY INQUIRY

1. PHYSICAL SYMPTOMS:

Pain
Burning
Itching
Numbness
Other odd sensations
Dizziness

These symptoms should be recorded if they are reported to be present (a) continuously or off and on for the past six months, and (b) have occurred at least twice during the preceding month.

Any unpleasant sensation, e.g. 'pulling sensation', 'current-like sensation', which fulfils the above criteria but has not been mentioned specifically in the Schedule, should be recorded in the box opposite *Other odd sensations* and specified below in the given space.

Indigestion
Weakness
Nausea
Wind

If the Pain, Burning, Itching, Numbness or Other odd sensations have been specifically reported for head, chest or anogenital region and on further inquiry reported to be present in the whole body, the symptom should be recorded *only* in the box under 'whole body'.

Any symptom besides Dizziness, Indigestion, Weakness, Nausea, Wind, which has not been specifically mentioned in the Schedule but otherwise fulfils the criteria mentioned above, should be specified in the given space.

Tiredness and exhaustion may be taken as synonyms for weakness. Besides fulfilling other criteria, weakness should only be recorded if it is present *even when the respondent is not working*.

Fits

These should be recorded when episodic convulsions in part or whole of the body and/or episodes of unconsciousness have occurred at least once during the preceding six months.

Note: This is only the provisional recording of the physical symptoms and fits. Anyone reported to have them must be further examined by a trained Psychiatrist, using Section II.

2. SLEEP AND APPETITE:

Sleep delay
Early waking
Generalised
sleeplessness

These symptoms should be recorded, only (a) if they have been reported to have occurred at least twice during the preceding week, and (b) the respondent can specify a point in time since when he is distressed by these. They should not be recorded if the respondent complains of 'always' having had them. Sleep delay should be recorded if the respondent definitely takes longer to sleep than before. Early waking should be recorded if the respondent definitely wakes up earlier than he used to.

Generalised sleeplessness should be recorded if the wakefulness is not of the nature of sleep delay or early waking, but is definitely more than it used to be before the respondent felt distressed by it.

Sleep delay and early waking may be recorded for the same person. However, if the sleep is disturbed during the rest of the night also, record only generalised sleeplessness.

Nightmares

This symptom should be recorded if the subject reports having been *woken up* by a *terrifying dream at least once* during the preceding week and on waking up suffered from palpitation, sweating and tremors.

Loss of appetite

This symptom should be recorded if the person reports to be *eating less well* 'these days'. Some people report being less hungry, but on further questioning admit that they eat as well as before. Loss of appetite should not be recorded in such cases.

3. MEMORY, CONCENTRATION, ETC.

This symptom should be recorded if the subject (a) can specify a point in time before which his memory was

Subjective forgetfulness	all right, and (b) can give a specific example of his forgetfulness.

Very often, Indian respondents report 'forgetfulness' when they really mean poor comprehension, poor concentration or pressure of ideas. An example of what they mean is therefore essential. Also the item should not be confused with chronic absentmindedness; a lifelong habit of forgetting to post letters should not be recorded as forgetfulness.

Poor concentration
This symptom should be recorded if the subject suffers from (a) an inability to keep his mind on what he is supposed to be doing, (b) can give a specific example of what he means, and (c) can specify a point in time before which his concentration was all right.

4. WORRIES, ANXIETIES, TENSIONS, ETC.:
Pathological worrying
Record this symptom, if (a) the worrying thoughts go round and round in the subject's head, and (b) he is unable to push them out of his mind at his will. Specific worries should be recorded in the given space.

Feeling of inferiority
Record this symptom if the subject (a) can give a specific example of the way he feels inferior to others, (b) the worrying thoughts go round and round in his head, and (c) he cannot push them out of his mind at will.

Situational anxiety
Phobia
Free-floating anxiety
Panic
Record these symptoms only if (a) a state of unpleasant apprehension is accompanied, (b) with at least one of the physical concomitants of anxiety like palpitation, tremors or sweating without reason.

Record Phobia, if (a) the fear is irrational, (b) the subject realises that it is irrational, but (c) is compelled to avoid the situation against his will.

Record Free-floating anxiety if the subject feels anxious or afraid without any reason or for very minor reasons (which did not make him anxious earlier) and has had such an experience at least twice during the preceding week.

Record Panic when the anxiety (situational or free-floating) was so great that the subject had to scream for help or run away from the situation and this occurred at least once during the preceding week.

Muscular tension
Record muscular tension if the subject reports a feeling of his body becoming tense, muscles becoming taut and 'nerves being pulled' at least twice during the preceding week, and the subject can describe the experience with an example.

Restlessness
Record restlessness if the subject reports such a state of mind at least twice during the preceding week.

Fugitive impulse
Record this symptom if the subject felt so restless that he wanted to leave everything and go away at least once during the preceding month.

Running away	Record this symptom if the subject reports having run away from the house because of restlessness, in full consciousness, at least once during the preceding six months.
Pressure of ideas	Record this symptom if the subject reports a state of mind when there were too many thoughts in his head, pressing on him, at least twice during the preceding week, and can give an example to illustrate his experience.
Poverty of thought	Record this symptom if the subject reports a state of mind when he felt his head being empty of thoughts, or blank, at least twice during the preceding week, and can give an example to illustrate his experience.
Irritability	Record this symptom if the subject reports being irritable without sufficient reason at least twice during the preceding week, and can give an example to illustrate his experience.
5. MOOD: Depression Dullness	Record these symptoms if the subject reports being sad or full 'most of the time' during the preceding week. Depression after a recent bereavement should not be recorded. Record it if the bereavement occurred more than three months ago.
Loss of interest	Record this symptom if the subject reports having lost interest in work, friends and relatives 'these days', and can give an example to illustrate his state of mind.
Feeling of incompetence	Record this symptom if the subject reports feeling 'these days' that he is a useless person who cannot accomplish much, and can give an example to illustrate his state of mind.
Suicidal feelings Suicidal attempt	Record Suicidal Feelings if the subject feels that life is not worth living, and has felt like ending his life, at least once during the previous month. Record Suicidal Attempt if the subject has really made any attempt to end his life at least once during the preceding six months. Anyone reporting Suicidal Attempt should be referred to the Psychiatrist for detailed examination.
Guilt feelings	Record this symptom if the subject feels that he has harmed someone or caused extreme distress to someone. Subject reporting Guilt Feelings should be referred to Psychiatrist to rule out any delusions.
Self blame	Record this symptom if the subject thinks he himself is responsible for his present state of mind (i.e. depression, loss of interest, etc.) and illustrates his feeling by saying that he has not led a good life, or by showing his Guilt Feelings. Record Self blame (previous life) if the subject claims that his present state is due to some bad actions in his previous life.

6. OBSESSIONS AND COMPULSIONS: — Record these symptoms if the subject suffers from a silly idea *repeatedly* entering his mind or is compelled to perform some unnecessary action repeatedly. The subject realises that such an idea or action is irrational but is unable to resist it and any attempt at resistance is attended by anxiety and tension.

7. SEXUAL PROBLEMS: — Record this symptom if the subject answers the related question in the affirmative, but refer the subject to Psychiatrist for further exploration.

Painful menstruation — Record this symptom if the subject generally suffers from pain during menstruation.

8. DELUSIONS AND HALLUCINA-TIONS:

Demon trouble — Record this symptom if the subject reports *ever* having been possessed or troubled in any other way by demon(s).

Ideas of persecution — Record this symptom if the subject reports having enemies who are working against him.

Hallucinations — Record this symptom if the subject reports *ever* having seen or heard things others cannot see or hear.

Special powers — Record this symptom if the person reports having spiritual or other special powers which others do not have.

Note: Presence of any of these symptoms suggests the possibility of delusions or hallucinations. Further detailed examination by a trained Psychiatrist is, however, necessary before their presence is confirmed.

SECTION II: DETAILED INQUIRY FROM THE SUBJECT

1. LIKELIHOOD OF PHYSICAL ILLNESS: — It is not always easy to decide whether the physical symptoms are due to physical illness or psychological factors. However, an experienced Psychiatrist can usually make a tentative judgement based on the way the symptoms are presented and the history of their development.

Physical symptoms of psychological origin are: (a) usually vague (b) very often exaggerated (the subject appearing to be healthier than he claims to be) and (c) generally accompanied by a history of psychological stress. None of these criteria is, however, definitive and the investigating Psychiatrist will have to call to his command the totality of his experience with such problems.

Try to make a judgement about the likelihood of physical illness and the code 'undetermined' should be used as sparingly as possible.

2. HYPOCHON- — Record this symptom if the subject is constantly pre-

DRIACAL PRE-
OCCUPATION:

occupied with his physical symptoms and cannot refrain from this subject during the rest of the interview. A hypochondriac exaggerates his discomfort, expressing unrealistic ideas on how his illness is going to cripple him. Dramatic words and gestures are frequently used to describe the complaints. Record the symptom if the above criteria are met even when physical illness has been recorded as 'not likely'.

3. CONVERSION
SYMPTOMS:

Hysterical paralysis
parasthesia
ataxia
blindness
deafness
aphonia
conversion (other)

Record these as present if on neurological examination these symptoms do not conform to a pattern expected with an organic defect.

4. FITS:

Epileptic
Hysterical

Epileptic fits usually follow a pattern which is repeated in each fit. The convulsions when present are of short duration. History of an aura preceeding the fit, injury or incontinence during the ictal period, postictal memory difficulties or transient neurological deficit support the diagnosis of epilepsy. Hysterical fits usually follow a bizarre pattern and may last for long periods. Pattern may be different in different fits. Injuries are rare. History of psychological stress is often reported.

5. SEXUAL
PROBLEMS:
(Unmarried male)

Sexual
preoccupation
Masturbation
worries
Night emission
worries
Other sexual
problems

To record the symptoms as present it is not sufficient for the subject to complain of sexual ideas, masturbation or night emissions; he must express his worries about these features.

Record in the given space what according to the subject the sexual problems might lead to.

6. SEXUAL
PROBLEMS:
(Married male)

Loss of sexual
desire

Record the symptom if the subject (a) has a subjective feeling of loss of sexual desire (b) has intercourse less often than he used to and (c) is worried about this problem, is unable to push the worrying thoughts out of his mind at will.

Impotence

Record the symptoms if the subject (under 50) is unable to have an erection during intercourse, is worried about this and is unable to push the worrying thoughts out of his mind.

Premature
ejaculation

Record the symptom if the subject feels that he gets seminal discharge too quickly, is worried about it and is unable to push the worrying thoughts out of his mind.

| Other sexual problems | Record them if the subject is worried about them and is unable to push the worrying thoughts out of mind. |

7. SEXUAL PROBLEMS: (for married females)

Definitions same as for married men.

Loss of sexual desire

Other sexual problems

Note: Record in the given space what the various sexual problems are due to.

8. DELUSIONS:

Guilt
Possession
Ideas of reference
Persecution (supernatural)
Persecution (human)
Grandiose
Systematisation
Acting out

Record these symptoms if the subject expresses beliefs which appear to be false to the investigator. A near relative must always be questioned (Section III) when delusions are recorded in this section.

Record ideas of reference if the subject suspects that the people are talking about him or referring to him in other ways but is not absolutely sure about this. The investigator must be convinced of the falsehood of this suspicion before the symptom is recorded.

Record 'Systematisation' of delusion if the subject has woven a story around his beliefs which would be rational enough if the delusional premises were to be true.

Record 'Acting out' of delusions if the subject has acted on the basis of his delusions, e.g. when a person fearing an attack from someone has lodged a complaint with the Police or assaulted the suspected person in self-defence.

9. HALLUCINA-TIONS:

Auditory
Visual
Olfactory
Gustatory
Tactile

Record hallucinations if the subject claims to have seen heard, tasted, smelt or felt sensations at least twice in the previous month, for which there is no objective evidence. The subject must be given an example before the symptoms are recorded.

Note: All Delusions and Hallucinations must be described in the given space(s).

SECTION III: DETAILED INQUIRY FROM A NEAR RELATIVE

1. SLEEP:

Oversleeping
Sleep delay
Early waking
Generalised sleeplessness

These symptoms should be recorded only if (a) they are reported to have occurred at least twice during the preceding week and (b) the respondent can specify a point in time before which the subject under investigation was free of these symptoms.

Oversleeping should be recorded if the subject sleeps longer than before and the respondent can illustrate his claim with an example. For example, the subject may sleep in the day when previously he did not, or he may be delayed at work because of having overslept. Definitions of Sleep Delay and Early Waking and Generalised

Sleeplessness are in Section I.

2. APPETITE:
Increased
Decreased

Record the symptom if the respondent claims that the subject eats *more* or *less* than before and can give an example to support his claim.

3. RESTLESSNESS:

Record the symptom if the respondent has observed at least twice during the preceding week that the subject is restless and cannot sit still in one place.

4. WANDERING
TENDENCEIS:

Record the symptom if the respondent claims that the subject wandered away from his home without reason at least once during the preceding month and came back after many hours or had to be brought back home. Just running up to the next house in a state of excitement should not be recorded as wandering tendency.

5. SLOWNESS:

Record slowness if the respondent has observed the subject to be generally slow during the preceding week and can support his claim with the help of an example.

6. BIZARRE
BEHAVIOUR:

Record Bizarre Behaviour if the respondent has observed that at least twice in the preceding week the subject performed actions which were fantastically strange, odd or in bad taste, and out of keeping with the social norms, e.g. singing and dancing in public, tearing clothes, etc. A person may behave in a bizarre fashion even when he is not excited.

7. EXCITEMENT:

Record Excitement if the respondent observed that at least twice in the preceding week the subject showed increased activity, running and jumping, waving arms, shouting or screaming and had to be held. In excitement the movements are more gross than in restlessness and there is no attempt on the subject's part to control himself.

8. STUPOR:

Record Stupor if the respondent observed that at least once in the preceding week the subject got into a state of immobility for more than an hour and did not respond to any outside stimulus during this period.

9. MOOD:
Irritability
Abusiveness
Violence
Suspiciousness
Depression
Elation

Record Irritability, Abusiveness or Violence if the respondent has observed that at least twice during the previous week the subject shows such behaviour without reason and can support his claim with an example.

Record Suspiciousness if the respondent has observed that the subject is becoming unjustifiably suspicious of others and can give an example to support his claim.

Record Depression if the respondent has observed the subject to be getting sad, morose and unhappy without sufficient reason.

Record Elation if the respondent has observed the subject to be strangely cheerful lately without reason. Respondent should be able to give example to support his claim.

An elated person looks cheerful, makes jokes and seems generally energetic. His cheerfulness is infectious and his jokes make others laugh, at least in the early stages.

10. SPEECH:

Too much ,
Too little
Muteness
Non-understandable

The terms need no further clarification. Record Too Much or Too Little Speech if the respondent has observed the subject to be showing such behaviour *lately* and can give example to support his claim.

Muteness should be recorded if it occurred at least once during the preceding week and lasted for at least one hour. A mute person still gives non-verbal responses while in Stupor there is a complete absence of any response.

Record Non-understandable speech if the respondent has observed the subject to be making meaningless statements at least twice during the previous week.

11. DELUSIONS:

Persecution
(human)
Persecution
(supernatural)
Grandeur
Possession
Guilt
Other delusions

Record Delusions if the respondent claims that the subject has beliefs which he *himself* knows to be false. Definitions of individual symptoms as in Section II.

12. HALLUCINA-
TIONS:

Record Hallucinations if the respondent has personal knowledge of the subject's claims to see or hear things or smell taste and feel sensations which the respondent believes do not exist in reality.

13. SENSORIUM:

Loss of memory
Disorientation

Record Loss of memory if the respondent has noticed the failing memory of the subject and can give examples to support his claim. Respondent should be able to specify a point in time before which the subject was all right.

Record Disorientation if the respondent claims that the subject is at many times unaware of his surroundings, is often unable to recognise the time of the day or his friends and relatives (not because of loss of eyesight or hearing).

14. SELF CARE:

Lack of self care
Complete
dependence

Record Lack of Self Care if the respondent claims that these days the subject is unable to eat without help, have bath without help or change his clothes without help.

Record complete dependance if the subject remains in bed and passes urine and motions in bed.

15. REDUCED
CAPACITY
TO WORK:

Record if the respondent claims that the subject does not work at all, or not as well as before, or not as well as others of his age and can give an example to support his claim.

16. SOCIAL WITH-

Record if the respondent claims that the subject is

DRAWAL AND
OVERSOCIA-
BILITY:

gradually withdrawing from his friends and relatives and does not mix with them as much as he used to. A life-long shy nature should not be recorded as social withdrawal.

Record Oversociability if the subject visits his friends and relatives much more than before, strikes friendships with strangers and these facts have been noticed as odd by the respondent.

17. RELIGIOSITY:
Increased
Decreased

Record if the subject visits temples and religious places much more or much less than before respectively and this fact has been noticed as odd by the respondent.

SECTION IV: OBSERVATION

1. SLOWNESS AND
UNDERACTIVITY:

Patient walks slowly into the room, makes very little movements during the interview and walks out as slowly afterwards. This is best highlighted if you compare his movements with those of the person(s) who came with him. If undecided ask him to shift from one chair to another or walk to the window and back, when the slowness will become obvious.

2. RESTLESSNESS:

Patient finds it difficult to sit still. He stands up frequently from the chair and may start pacing the floor. There is, however, an apparent attempt on patient's part to control himself.

3. EXCITEMENT:

Patient runs and jumps, waves arms, shouts or screams; may have to be held. Movements much more gross than in 'restlessness'. There is no attempt on patient's part to control himself.

4. BIZARRE
BEHAVIOUR:

Patient indulges in behaviour fantastically strange and inappropriate, like singing and dancing in response to questions, taking off clothes, etc. This may accompany excitement but not necessarily so.

5. CATATONIC
MOVEMENTS:

These should be directly tested for. Omit the examination if the patient tells his story himself, speaks rationally and is generally co-operative.

(a) Echopraxia:

At times during the interview, slowly raise your arms above the head. The patient will imitate the movements.

(b) Negativism:

Deliberately perform different movements in front of the patient. He will carry out the opposite movements.

(c) Ambitendence:

At times during the interview extend your hand as if to hold the patient's hand. He will first extend the hand automatically and then withdraw.

(d) Flexibilitas
cerea:

Raise the patient's arm above his head without advising him to keep it there. He will keep the arm in that position for at least 15 seconds before bringing it down.

(e) Passivity
phenomenon:

Put slight pressure on patient's neck and he will bend it completely.

(f) Echolalia:	Say a few words with different intonation and inflection of the voice. Patient will repeat the words with same intonation and inflection.
6. EXCESSIVE PRE-OCCUPATION:	Patient is lost in thoughts. It is difficult, though not impossible to arouse his attention. Questions may have to be repeated.
7. DISTRACTIBILITY:	Patient is co-operative but he is unable to give sustained attention to the interview, as he is constantly distracted by outside events, e.g. objects or other people in the room, people passing outside the window, etc.
8. STUPOR:	Patient sits, stands or lies down absolutely still without blinking eyes for long periods, and does not respond to questions, touch or deliberately made loud noises like clapping of the hands. Face is usually expressionless and saliva may be seen dripping from the corner of the mouth.
9. BLUNTED AFFECT:	Patient's face is expressionless and the voice has monotonous intonation and inflection throughout the interview.
10. INCONGRUOUS AFFECT:	Emotion is shown but has no relation with the topic. Patient may giggle when talking of a sad event and vice versa.
11. HOSTILE IRRITABILITY:	Patient is un-co-operative, insulting, abusive. He may want to leave the room and is generally angry.
12. HYPOMANIC MOOD:	Patient is unduly cheerful and confident. He makes jokes and tall claims. Generally entertaining.
13. HISTRIONIC:	Patient gives the story of his symptoms in a dramatic manner. For example he indulges in mime to show how 'the pain travels from stomach upwards to produce heat in the head' putting up an 'exaggerated miserable expression' or a 'resigned martyr's expression'.
14. TOO MUCH SPEECH:	Patient talks incessantly, spontaneously, rapidly but meaningfully.
15. TOO LITTLE SPEECH:	No spontaneous speech. Patient answers questions in monosyllables but to the point.
16. MUTISM:	No speech at all.
17. INCOHERENT SPEECH:	Though the patient uses ordinary words he uses them out of context. Ununderstandable.
18. IRRELEVANT SPEECH:	Patient does not answer questions to the point though the sentences are understandable.
19 FLIGHT OF IDEAS:	Patient shifts from topic to topic usually in a spontaneous delivery. Clang association common.
20. DELUSIONS AND HALLUCINATIONS:	As in Section II.

21. DISORIENTATION: Record if the patient fails to give satisfactory answers to any of the given questions.

SECTION V

EXCESSIVE ALCOHOL
DRUGS
BAD HABITS:
It is difficult to have an objective definition for these items of behaviour since the cultural factors as well as the family tolerance would play such a large part in determining what is acceptable and what is not.

Record these items as present if the subject indulges in them much more than others and is a source of nuisance to his family and others.

LEGAL
INVOLVEMENT: Definition, self evident.

Definitions for other items as in Section III.

Appendix II

SOCIAL FUNCTIONING
QUESTIONNAIRE

Introduction: You have told me about your problem. Now I want to ask you a few more questions:

Q.1 Do you feel you cannot cope with your work because of these troubles? Do you find it difficult to meet people and fulfil your social duties? (Can you give an example?)

> *Inability to cope:*   Yes/No

For Males:

Q.2 Do you do any work during the monsoons? (Are you working during the present monsoon season?) (What work do you do?) (How many hours a day do you work?)

> *Work during monsoons:* 0 = Nil
> 1 = Up to 2 hours
> 2 = 3–4 hours
> 3 = 5–6 hours
> 4 = 7 +

Q.3 I will ask you about some odd jobs around the house. Tell me if you do any of these at all? (How often?)

	Up to 2 times a week	3–5 times a week	6–7 times a week
Feeding the cattle with fodder and water	....	....	....
Watering the vegetable garden	....	....	....
Bringing provisions for home	....	....	....
Clearing the cobwebs in the house?	....	....	....

For Females:

Q. I will ask you about house work. Do you do any of these jobs at home? (How many times in the last week?)

	Up to 2 times a week	3–5 times a week	6–7 times a week
Cooking the rice	....	....	....
Cooking the vegetables	....	....	....
Grinding the coconut	....	....	....
Serving the food	....	....	....
Washing the dishes	....	....	....
Sweeping the floor	....	....	....

Q.4 How often do you go to the 'town' in the evenings? (How many times did you go last week?)

Visits to the town: 0 = Nil
1 = Once
2 = 2–4 times
3 = 5–6 times
4 = Every day

Q.5 In the last month how many times have you been to pictures, festivals, cock fights, folk drama, Udipi or Coondapoor? (approximately ......?)

Entertainments: 0 = Nil
1 = 1–2 times
2 = 3–4 times
3 = 5–6 times
4 = 7–8 times
5 = 9–10 times
6 = 10 + times

Q.6 In the last month how many times have you been to the temple? (approximately ....?)

Visits to temple: 0 = Nil
1 = 1–2 times
2 = 3–4 times
3 = 5–6 times
4 = 7–8 times
5 = 9–10 times
6 = 10 + times

Q.7 In the last month how many times have you been to a demon shrine? (approximately ....?)

Visits to demon shrines: 0 = Nil
1 = 1–2 times
2 = 3–4 times
3 = 5–6 times
4 = 7–8 times
5 = 9–10 times
6 = 10 + times

From married people:

Q.8 In the last month how many times have you been to the 'town' .... relatives .... or pictures, etc. with your husband/wife?

Visits out with spouse: 0 = Nil
1 = 1–2 times
2 = 3–4 times
3 = 5–6 times
4 = 7–8 times
5 = 9–10 times
6 = 10 + times

Q.9 How often did you have sexual intercourse during the last month?

Sexual intercourse: 0 = Nil
1 = 1–2 times
2 = 3–4 times
3 = 5–6 times

4 = 7–8 times
5 = 9–10 times
6 = 10 + times

Q.10 Before children go to bed do you play with them at all?
(How many times last week?)

Playing with children: 0 = Nil
1 = Once
2 = 2–4 times
3 = 5–6 times
4 = Every day

REFERENCES

Bogardus, E. S. (1959). *Social Distance*. Los Angeles: E. S. Bogardus

Carstairs, G. M. (1957). *The Twice-Born: a Study of a Community of High-caste Hindus*. London: Hogarth Press

Carstairs, G. M. (1956), 'Hinjra and Jiryan: two derivatives of Hindu attitudes to sexuality', *Brit. J. med. Psychol.*, **29**, 5

Cooper, J. E., Kendall, R. E., Gurland, B. J., Sharpe, L., Copeland, J. R. M., and Simon, R. (1972). *Psychiatric Diagnosis in New York and London*. London: Oxford Univ. Press (Maudsley Monograph No. 20)

Dean, S. R., and Thong, D. (1972). 'Shamanism versus psychiatry in Bali, 'Isle of Gods', *Amer. J. Psychiatry*, **129**, 59–62

Dube, K. C. (1970). 'A study of prevalence of mental illness in Uttar Pradesh, India', *Acta psychiat. scand.*, **46**, 327

Giel, R., and Van Luijk, J. N. (1969). 'Psychiatric morbidity in a small Ethiopian town', *Brit. J. Psychiat.*, **115**, 149

Goldberg, D. P., Eastwood, M. R., Kedward, H. B., and Shepherd, M. (1970). 'A standardised psychiatric interview for use in community surveys', *Brit. J. prev. soc. Med.*, **24**, 18–23

Illich, I. (1974). *Medical Nemesis: the Expropriation of Health*. London: Calder & Boyars

Kapur, R. L., Kapur, Malavika, and Carstairs, G. M. (1974). 'Indian Psychiatric Interview Schedule (IPIS)', *Social Psychiatry*, **9**, 61–69.

Kapur, R. L., Kapur, Malavika, and Carstairs, G. M. (1974). 'Indian Psychiatric Survey Schedule (IPSS)', *Social Psychiatry*, **9**, 71–76

Kessel, W. I. N. (1965). 'Are International Comparisons Timely?', in Acheson, R. M. (editor), *Comparability in International Epidemiology*. New York: Milbank Memorial Fund

King, M. (1966). *Medical Care in Developing Countries*. Oxford Univ. Press (East Africa)

Kreitman, N., Sainsbury, P., Morrissey, J., Towers, J., and Scrivener, J. (1961). 'The reliability of psychiatric assessment: an analysis', *J. ment. Sci.*, **107**, 887

Leighton, Dorothea C., Harding, J. S., Macklin, D. S., Macmillan, A. M., and Leighton, A. H. (1963). *The Character of Danger: Psychiatric Symptoms in Selected Communities*. New York: Basic Books

Leighton, A. H., Lambo, T. A., Hughes, C. C., Leighton, Dorothea C., Murphy, Jane M., and Macklin, D. B. (1963). *Psychiatric Disorder among the Yoruba*. Ithaca, N. Y.: Cornell Univ. Press

Mahar, Pauline M. (1959). 'A Multiple Scaling Technique for Caste Ranking', *Man in India*, **39**, 127–147

Mandlebaum, D. G. (1938). 'Polyandry in Kota Society', *Amer. Anthropologist*, **40**, 574–583

Mandlebaum, D. G. (1955). 'The world and the world-view of the Kota', in Marriott, M. (editor), *Village India*, pp. 223–254. Chicago Univ. Press

Mandlebaum, D. G. (1956). 'The Kotas in their social setting', in Singer, M. (editor), *Introduction to the civilization of India*. Chicago Univ. Press

Mandlebaum, D. G. (1970), *Society in India*, Vols. I & II. Berkeley: Univ. of California Press

Mathew, G. K. (1971). 'Measuring need and evaluating services', in MacLachlan, G. (editor), *Portfolio for Health Problems and Progress in Medical Care*. Oxford: Foundation Press

Mechanic, D. (1972). *Public Expectations in Health Care: Essays on the Changing Organization of Health Services*. New York: Interscience (Wiley)

Neki, J. S., and Kapur, R. L. (1963). 'Social stratification of psychiatric patients', *Indian J. Psychiat.*, 5, 76

Pasamanick, B., Dinitz, S., and Lefton, M. (1959). 'Psychiatric orientation and its relation to diagnosis and treatment in a mental hospital', *Amer. J. Psychiat.*, 116, 127–132

Schmidt, K. E. (1967). 'Mental Health Services in a developing country of South-East Asia (Sarawak)', in Freeman, H. L., and Farndale, J. (editors), *New aspects of the mental health service*. Oxford: Pergamon Press

Smith, D. H., and Inkeles, A. (1966). 'The O.M. Scale: a comparative socio-psychological measure of individual modernity', *Sociometry*, 29, 353–377

Srole, L., Langner, T. S., Michael, S. T., Opler, M. K., and Rennie, T. A. C. (1962). *Mental Health in the Metropolis: The Mid-town Manhattan Study*. New York: McGraw-Hill

Thacore, V. R. (1973). *Mental Illness in an Urban Community*. Allahabad: United Publishers

Torrey, E. F. (1973). 'Is schizophrenia universal? An open question?', *Schiz. Bull.*, 7, 53–57

WHO: Regional Office for South East Asia (1971). *Report of a Seminar on the Organization and future needs of Mental Health Services*. New Delhi: SEA/Ment.19

World Health Organization (1973). *Organizational Study on Methods of Promoting the Development of Basic Health Services*. Geneva: Official Records of WHO, No. 206, 103–115

World Health Organization (1975). *The Organization of Mental Health Services in the Developing Countries. Report of an Expert Committee on Mental Health*. Geneva: WHO Technical Report Series, No. 564.

INDEX